99 WRITING PROMPTS TO CRAFT
A TALE OF TERROR AND DARKNESS

WRITE A HORROR NOVEL

Erik Patterson
@yourdailywritingprompt

ADAMS MEDIA
New York Amsterdam/Antwerp London Toronto Sydney/Melbourne New Delhi

Adams Media
An Imprint of Simon & Schuster, LLC
100 Technology Center Drive
Stoughton, MA 02072

First Adams Media trade paperback edition May 2026

Interior design by Priscilla Yuen
Interior images © Adobe Stock;
Simon & Schuster, LLC

Manufactured in the United States of America

1 2026

Library of Congress Cataloging-in-Publication Data has been applied for.

ISBN 978-1-5072-2613-1
ISBN 978-1-5072-2614-8 (ebook)

DEDICATION

For my incredible family.

ACKNOWLEDGMENTS

In middle school, I feverishly read every Stephen King book, devouring all the twists and terrifying turns, so I must begin by acknowledging a deep debt to Mr. King for showing me how fun it is to be scared. Thank you to all the writers I've met on TikTok, and the community we've formed there (with a special shout-out to Brujadepi, Saige, Shar, Leila, Tardis, Julia, Katie Keeley, Simply Ray, Marcus, Stephanie, and Bones). I am ever grateful for my wonderful editor, Natalie McGregor, who is the absolute best. Thank you to everyone at Simon & Schuster and Adams Media. Jennifer Kristal, thank you for your keen eyes and thoughtful notes. And, as always, a huge thank you to Sherry Angel.

CONTENTS

INTRODUCTION

A delivery driver makes a stop at a perilous location and is now being hunted for sport.

A single woman connects with a stranger online, but he has literal skeletons in his closet.

A family discovers their new home is haunted by vengeful spirits who vow to retake their *property.*

Intrigued? Readers turn to horror stories to face their greatest fears. These are worlds where evil lurks in every shadow, good people succumb to their worst impulses, and heroes don't always win. Great horror stories have something to say about the human condition: They acknowledge that the real world can be horrific. Magnifying these horrors through the lens of ghosts, demons, and monsters gives readers a catharsis that's totally unique to the horror genre. *Write a Horror Novel* will take all the fear out of your writing process so you can focus on scaring your readers.

Whether you've already written a horror novel, short story, or other creative work and just want to generate ideas, or you're an unseasoned scare master, the prompts in this book will help you access your most terrifying storytelling instincts. Use these tools to invent a unique setting, indelible characters, and an unpredictable plot. Part 1 of *Write a Horror Novel* will give you the resources you need to create characters a reader will follow to frightful places—and to build an eerily vivid world that supports the themes and ideas you're exploring.

Part 2 will help you bring your vision to life on the page. You'll find thirty-three chapters, each focused on a different horror trope (a common theme or literary device), such as Unseen Monster, Evil Twin, and The Final Girl, among many others. You'll explore each trope through various prompts that will get you thinking about character backstory, thematic intention, terrifying twists and turns, and how to use your unique perspective to make the formulaic elements of the horror genre feel fresh again. Ultimately, each of the ninety-nine prompts will get you writing, help you create genuinely frightening shocks for your readers, and make it easy to flesh out scenes and characters. For example, you'll:

- Learn how to use conflict to raise the stakes of your story.
- Examine your connection to your favorite scary stories, and mine those fears in a way that makes them feel totally new.
- Broaden your characters' perspectives by having them face off against a monster or demon they don't believe in.
- And more!

Remember: Readers connect to stories through characters they can identify with. Even if the horror elements in your story are outrageous and unbelievable, your reader will go along with just about any scenario if they recognize and empathize with your protagonist. So, make them care about your characters and the world they inhabit. Think of each prompt as a way to discover who your protagonist is and how they interact with their surroundings. Even if you don't use a scene in your final draft, these exercises often serve an important purpose, such as unlocking the lore of your world or revealing the motivations of your characters. So, whether you're writing a novel, fan fiction, screenplay, short story, RPG campaign, or comic, be bold! Get ready to lead your readers into a harrowing and spooky tale. And don't be surprised when you discover that dwelling in a *fictional* horror story can be fun!

HOW TO USE THIS BOOK

Horror stories give readers a chance to indulge in their most gruesome fantasies and explore the root of their deepest fears. Making a deliberate decision to *terrify yourself* might seem absurd to some, but horror lovers will say those people are missing out on an emotional release unlike any other. The act of writing horror is a journey of its own, but thankfully it doesn't have to be a truly frightening one. At least, not with the help of this book.

Think about what scares you most and put it on the page. Anne Rice famously wrote *Interview with the Vampire* in response to the loss of her young daughter; she channeled her grief into a story about a young girl who becomes an immortal vampire. By taking a real-life fear held by many (an unspeakable loss) and adding a horror element (vampires), she created a timeless story that allows readers to safely face their own emotional responses to love and loss. This opening section of *Write a Horror Novel* illustrates how you can best use writing prompts designed specifically for this genre. First, you'll find a detailed description of how each prompt functions and how the prompts can provide a structure for your writing sessions. Then you'll find some basic rules to follow while you're writing. You'll receive some pointers on how to begin your writing journey, as well as how to tie everything together in the end. But before we get to the prompts, let's think about what tropes are and why this book is built around them.

☞ Navigate the Prompts and Trope Chapters

Each chapter that follows offers writing prompts related to a specific horror trope—a consistent and recurring theme/element that horror readers expect and search for. Your challenge is to take these familiar plot devices to unexpected places. For example, if the characters in your story discover a Haunted Object, how can you have them unlock the object's powers in a way that readers have never seen before? Or if your characters suspect an evil demon has entered their home, what new and unusual tactics might they use to uncover the horrifying truth that They're Living in the Walls? Or how might you orchestrate a Ritual Killing that surprises your readers as much as (or more than) your protagonist?

Just as Hannibal Lecter savors a meal over many courses, you will absorb the prompts in this book in small bites as you make your way through several sections: The Scenario section provides the setup for a scene, with malleable plot elements for you to consider before you begin writing. Remember: You can alter the details described in the scenario any way you see fit so they apply to the specifics of your story. The Brainstorm section has you interrogate your own characters, clarifying what you should know about them before you dive into the new scene you're about to write. The Write section contains the prompt itself. The Optional Elements to Include section is a great resource when you feel stuck; grab a random optional element, incorporate it into your scene, and keep writing! The remaining sections, Horror Twist and Callbacks, provide even more inspiration, and if you focus on a different supplemental section each time you use a prompt, it will feel new again, so you can reuse each exercise multiple times. As a bonus, each prompt has a line of dialogue as its header; if you're not sure how to find your way into a new scene, use these starter lines and see where they take you.

Each chapter features three longer prompts, followed by five additional Quick Writes prompts. These quick prompts ask you to write continuously for 15 minutes, giving your unconscious mind a chance to take over. Imagine you're trapped in a serial killer's basement and you realize he left the door unlocked. You'd make a mad dash for freedom, scrambling out of his house as quickly as possible, right? Do these Quick Writes with that energy. Don't plan or prepare—just write! Surprise yourself with the character discoveries you make.

Now that you have a better idea of how to approach the prompts in this book, let's lay down some rules for writing a horror novel. These rules will become a vital element of your writing process; come back to these words of advice whenever you feel creatively stuck.

☞ The Rules

One of the most common themes of the horror genre is the danger of what's unknown. Think of the following rules as a set of powerful tools that will help you take charge of the writing process so you can keep that danger on the page in ways that will thrill your readers.

The Dr. Jekyll and Mr. Hyde Rule

Two writers exist within every novelist: a good one and a bad one. And you may not be able to access your best writing if you don't allow yourself to write badly first. Here's another secret: You cannot rewrite a blank page, but you can always make bad writing better. So, channel your inner Mr. Hyde and be very bad. Then let Dr. Jekyll come to the rescue.

The *American Psycho* Rule

The greatest joys of writing come from thinking about your story, experimenting with what works, and putting in the time to get it right. Only psychos use AI to do their thinking, so don't be a Patrick Bateman. The stories you come up with on your own are, and always will be, better than anything your computer could create.

The *Carrie* Rule

Carrie White probably would have been a lot happier if she didn't always listen to her mom. It's healthy to think for yourself and question the things people in authority tell you to do. So, if you prefer to focus on some elements of a prompt and ignore others, that's totally fine. You can always come back to the same prompt later and work with it differently.

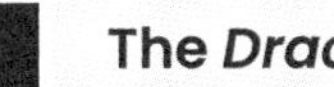

The *Dracula* Rule

Vampires are persistent. If they need to ensnare a new victim to prove loyalty to their master, they won't stop hunting until they've achieved their goal. Similarly, a book doesn't get written overnight. Create a routine, stay consistent, put all your blood, sweat, and tears into it, and, above all, keep writing. Before you know it, you'll have a first draft.

The Metamorphosis Rule

Take care of yourself while you're writing. Go outside and get some sun, drink eight glasses of water a day, and be active. Taking a brisk walk in the middle of a writing session will help you see your story with fresh eyes. Don't be a Gregor Samsa and overwork yourself to the point where you feel like a disgusting insect.

The *Misery* Rule

Annie Wilkes didn't like how novelist Paul Sheldon finished his book, so she made him change it. Similarly, if you don't like specific details in a prompt, you can always change them to make the prompt work better for the story you're writing. Annie wouldn't tolerate a detail that made her miserable, and you shouldn't either! Feel free to adjust prompts to your liking.

These rules are an important place to start, but ignore them as you see fit; just like your characters, you'll learn to adapt to the world you're building, and what's a horror novel without a few surprising twists and turns?

Start Writing

It's time to grab a notebook, or open a new document on your computer, and write. If you like to outline, look for prompts that address specific needs in your story. If you're more of a figure-out-the-story-as-you-go type of writer, pick a trope you love and start there. There's no limit to how many prompts you can use; each one could lead you in countless directions. Whenever you're struggling with writer's block, pick a prompt at random and let it guide you toward a new scene.

☞ Putting It All Together

Let's be real: You're writing horror, which means many of your characters won't make it to the end of your story. But there's one person who will, without a shadow of a doubt, get to the final page. You. So relax. Use the prompts in this book on a regular basis, and eventually you'll have a first draft. There is no particular order in which you should complete these prompts. Nor is there just one way to approach the writing process. The more you write, the more you'll discover and fine-tune your writing routine. Putting it all together looks different for everyone. The important thing is to figure out what works best for you—and do it!

You'll define your story's world and characters in Part 1 of *Write a Horror Novel*. Then you'll combine them with the conflicts, plot elements, shocking reveals, and complicated backstories you dream up in Part 2. You can always add details as you revise. Send your characters on a horrifying journey where they face their greatest fears, navigate a landscape full of monsters and things that go bump in the night, and struggle to stay alive in a world where death is around every corner. This book gives you a framework to create the ultimate horror novel. You have a unique voice. Use it now. Write a story that makes you afraid to turn out the lights; it's bound to do the same to your readers.

PART 1

FOUNDATIONS OF HORROR

One of the reasons readers love horror fiction is because it's a safe way to explore their most forbidden desires and to confront their deepest fears. As you're brainstorming your story, look inward and ask yourself what you're most afraid of. Chances are other people share those fears. Whether you're writing about a serial killer, vampires, ghosts, demonic possession, or something else, you can give your own complicated emotions to your characters.

Writing horror can be an act of pure joy, because it lets you process your fears from the safety of your own laptop. *Write a Horror Novel* will help you balance good storytelling and important themes as you develop a gripping plot that puts complicated characters into dangerous situations. Make your readers care about your characters and they will follow them down every dark alley, into every sketchy basement, and through the most perverse madman's life-or-death maze.

When you find that perfect balance of heart-pounding fear and tense relief that a horror novel begs for, your readers will white-knuckle their way through your book, desperate to find out what each new chapter reveals. Use the Character Creation Cheat Sheet in the following pages to clarify how your characters navigate their worst nightmares and what emotional qualities contribute to their ultimate survival.

Next you will find tools for building the horror world of your story. Pick a setting and answer the questions in the Worldbuilding Questionnaire. As you imagine the challenges your characters face in this dark and disturbing world, your story will come to life.

Creating Your Characters

Horror often takes place in an environment much like the real world. That's part of what makes these stories so unsettling; readers can imagine the same horrors happening to them. The motifs that characterize these stories turn up just as often in the average person's psyche, such as fear of death, anxiety about unknown or foreign forces, and a wariness of the sway religion holds on society.

The people who inhabit these worlds are complicated and morally flawed. They have everyday problems they're trying to deal with when bigger issues arise. Before they've even encountered the demons (either literal or metaphorical) that they must face, they should come across as well-rounded and real. That's where the Character Creation Cheat Sheet comes in. Select an Archetype (a universally recognized character type) from the following section, and a couple of adjectives from the Prime Characteristics section. Then add some flair with a Horror Fiction Type. It's a simple formula:

Archetype + Prime Characteristic + Horror Fiction Type = A Compelling Character

Use this for your main characters, supporting characters, and antagonists. Then, perhaps write a short biography for each character, letting each chosen element shine.

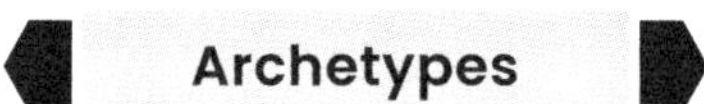

Archetypes

Several archetypal characters pop up time and again in horror fiction. An archetype is an easily recognizable character type that embodies a specific aspect of the human experience. An archetypal character will feel to your readers like someone they've seen before—someone they inherently understand. It's your job to add color and original details to make the character unique. Here is a non-exhaustive list of some of the archetypes that populate horror fiction:

The Final Girl: A protagonist of a horror story who is the ultimate survivor. Since she's the survivor at the end of your story, she must confront the killer all by herself. She wasn't always so strong, but she's been hardened by everything she's been through. Ultimately, she's ready to face anything.

The Monster: Horror antagonists come in many forms. They can be humans (serial killers, psychos); spirits (ghosts, demons); the undead (zombies, vampires); creatures (aliens, cryptids); or even part of the natural world (killer plants, malevolent fog). The Monster is in stark opposition to your protagonist.

The Familiar: Someone who helps the antagonist. They often play an official role as your antagonist's assistant. Their allegiance is always with the dark side. They will sacrifice themself to secure a win against your protagonist, if necessary.

The Fallen One: A good character who turns evil. This is often your protagonist's best friend, someone your protagonist trusts implicitly—until they're changed by an outside force. Once corrupted, they pose a grave threat to your protagonist.

The Authority Figure: This could be a cop, a detective, or even a librarian. This is a character who seeks answers and wants to use their position of power to do good.

The Possessed: This character has been to hell and back, literally. They are being controlled by supernatural forces, and they struggle to break free and act autonomously.

The Guide: This character is a mentor or ally to your protagonist. What they lack in people skills they make up for in research, data, and education. The Guide often ends up dying prematurely, but hopefully not before sharing their knowledge with your protagonist.

The Harbinger: This is a character who warns your protagonist of the dangers that await them if they pursue The Monster. They might be a loved one of The Monster's victims, or they might have survived an attack by The Monster themself. Their warning is often cast aside.

The Best Friend: This is your protagonist's greatest ally. They act as a sounding board, play devil's advocate, and are willing to accompany your protagonist into a dangerous situation. They're often one of the first to die, but their death will motivate your protagonist to keep fighting.

When you're building characters for your horror novel, think of these archetypes as blank canvases. It's your job to sketch in the details by giving them specific traumas, hopes, secrets, dreams, and idiosyncrasies. The best way to figure out who your characters are is by thinking about what they need.

Prime Characteristics

Many victims in horror stories have their individuality stripped away by evil forces. As a writer, your job is to imbue your characters with so much individuality that your reader falls in love with them and mourns them when they're gone. Use this list of prime character traits as a baseline to help you determine how your characters behave.

ADVENTUROUS	DISGRUNTLED	INTUITIVE	ROUGH
AGGRESSIVE	DRUNK	JADED	RUTHLESS
AGITATED	EMOTIONAL	JEALOUS	SADISTIC
ALIENATED	ENVIOUS	JUDGMENTAL	SAVAGE
ANGRY	EUPHORIC	LARCENOUS	SECRETIVE
ANXIOUS	FAITHLESS	LITIGIOUS	SELFISH
BARBARIC	FEARFUL	LOGICAL	SEXY
BITTER	FEROCIOUS	LOYAL	SHARP
BLITZED	FLIRTATIOUS	LUSTFUL	SNEAKY
BRAVE	FORGIVING	MEAN	STOIC
CAREFUL	FRUSTRATED	MESSY	STRONG
CAUSTIC	GLOOMY	MOODY	STUBBORN
CHARMING	GREEDY	NAIVE	TACTLESS
COLD-HEARTED	GRIZZLED	NARCISSISTIC	TEMPERAMENTAL
COMPETITIVE	GUARDED	NEEDY	THREATENING
CONFUSED	GUILT-RIDDEN	OBEDIENT	TOUGH
CONTROLLING	HARSH	OBNOXIOUS	UNCARING
COOPERATIVE	HATEFUL	OBSESSIVE	UNRELIABLE
CRUEL	HAUNTED	PARANOID	UNSETTLED
DAMAGED	HOTHEADED	PASSIONATE	VENGEFUL
DARK	HUNGRY	PERSISTENT	VIOLENT
DECEITFUL	IMMORAL	PETTY	VIRTUOUS
DEPENDABLE	IMPATIENT	RATIONAL	VULNERABLE
DESPERATE	IMPROPER	REGRETFUL	WARY
DISCREET	IMPURE	RESENTFUL	WEAK-WILLED
DISGRACED	INSECURE	RESILIENT	WICKED

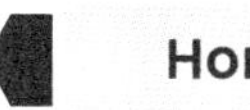

Horror Fiction Types

One of the scariest things about horror stories is they can happen to anyone, anywhere, at any time. The characters in these stories come from all walks of life, with all kinds of jobs and lifestyles. Use this list of types to create a dynamic cast of characters.

- ANIMATOR
- ARTIST
- ASSASSIN
- BABYSITTER
- BARTENDER
- BILLIONAIRE
- BODYGUARD
- CHEERLEADER
- COP
- COUNSELOR
- CRIME SCENE PHOTOGRAPHER
- CRIMINAL
- CULT LEADER
- DANCER
- DETECTIVE
- DIETITIAN
- ELECTRICIAN
- EMT
- EXTERMINATOR
- FIREFIGHTER
- FORENSIC SPECIALIST
- FORTUNE TELLER
- GAS STATION ATTENDANT
- HACKER
- HOARDER
- IMAGE CONSULTANT
- INFLUENCER
- INMATE
- JOCK
- JUDGE
- MINISTER
- MORTICIAN
- NEIGHBOR
- NERD
- NICE GUY
- PIG FARMER
- PRIEST
- PRISONER
- PSYCHIATRIST
- RARE BOOK COLLECTOR
- RECRUITER
- REPORTER
- SCHOLAR
- SECURITY GUARD
- SHOPKEEPER
- STONER
- STUDENT
- TATTOO ARTIST
- TECH BRO
- THIEF
- TRUCK DRIVER
- VALET
- VETERINARIAN
- VIRGIN
- WAITRESS
- WEAPONEER
- WRITER

Now that you have a basic understanding of whose story you're telling, use the next section of this book to begin creating the world they live in. Character development and worldbuilding feed off each other, which means you'll continue bringing your characters to life as you define their environment.

Worldbuilding

What are your characters afraid of? How do these fears affect the way they navigate the world? The act of worldbuilding in horror is more about elucidating what your story feels like, rather than how it looks. It's almost like creating a story from the inside out: You create a world of horror by defining the emotional, internal, and psychological landscape inhabited by your characters.

When you grasp the terrors your characters will encounter, you can use that knowledge to build a world around them. In what environments are these fears most likely to manifest themselves? How can the world of your story heighten these fears? Let your characters loose in an environment where their fears are bound to fester.

As you're writing, it's especially important to have a clear sense of the rules of your world. What powers or weaknesses does your antagonist possess? What do they want? What are they driven by? How can they be killed? Once you've established how this world functions, make sure you stay consistent as you develop your characters and story.

But before you dig into those details, it's helpful to clarify what kind of horror novel you're writing. There are a number of great options to consider, including the following subgenres.

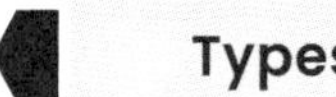

Types of Worlds

Which of these horror subgenres applies best to your story? These are some shortcuts to get you started on your worldbuilding process. Just select a category and Potential Starter Setting from this list:

Body Horror: Your characters suffer from mutilations, horrible transformations, and unusual, often grotesque, body manipulations. This is a world of excess and gore. *Potential Starter Settings:* an underground operating room, a high-end plastic surgery office, a dungeon.

Occult Horror: Your characters get caught up in a world of witches, mysterious magic, and demonic possession. Paganism, spells, and other mystical forces are the norm. *Potential Starter Settings:* a restaurant parking lot, the kitchen at an old bed-and-breakfast, a liquor store back office.

Paranormal Horror: Your characters face off against ghosts, werewolves, vampires, and other supernatural monsters. *Potential Starter Settings:* a cemetery, the attic of an old Victorian home, a church courtyard.

Psychological Horror: Your characters confront manipulation, gaslighting, and emotional terrors as a psychologically savvy villain weaponizes trauma from their past. *Potential Starter Settings:* a psychologist's office, a remote hotel, a prison cell.

Slasher Horror: A killer with preternatural strength and deeply held obsessions hunts your characters. There is always a blade, which makes these stories bloody and violent. *Potential Starter Settings:* an old farm, a morgue, a mall food court.

Survival Horror: Your characters must survive in the wild while facing extreme elements. And they might not be alone: Someone, or something, might be out there hunting them. *Potential Starter Settings:* a research station in Antarctica, the bottom of a well, a trail that seems to lead to nowhere.

Zombie Horror: Your characters live in a postapocalyptic world where the dead walk the Earth. They're trying to recreate a semblance of a normal life, while doing everything they can to survive another day. *Potential Starter Settings:* an abandoned warehouse, an airport, an office building.

Try this to help you get going:

Carry a notebook or journal with you wherever you go. Whenever an idea about the world of your story pops into your head, write it down.

Worldbuilding Questionnaire

The questions on this list are designed to get you thinking about how deep and complex the world of your story can be. Use these questions to begin exploring what your world looks like, but don't feel limited by this list. Follow any paths these questions send you down.

- What scary myths, legends, and ghost stories do the people in the world of your story commonly believe?
- Think about the physical spaces in the world of your story: If your protagonist was running away from an evil creature, what would be the best hiding places?

- What kind of lore surrounds your antagonist? What's the worst thing your antagonist has ever done, and how much does the average person know about this evildoer?
- Do people use cell phones in this world? How would your protagonist try to get help if they were stranded in the middle of nowhere?
- Can your antagonist appear in visions, dreams, or hallucinations?
- Is the world of your story more rural, suburban, or industrial?
- What is your protagonist's daily routine? How might your antagonist disrupt the general ordinariness of their world?
- List five ordinary objects your protagonist might find in his environment that he could use as makeshift weapons.
- Does your story take place on land that was stolen, haunted, or cursed?
- What smells, tastes, and sounds do you associate with this world?

Feel free to add your own questions to this list.

Once you've decided which horror subgenre best fits your story, do some freewriting to imagine how your characters fit in this world. But there's no need to figure out every detail right now. You will continue building your world through the prompts in the next part of this book. It's time to write!

PART 2

PROMPTS TO INSPIRE

In this part of the book, you'll find a variety of writing prompts paired with horror tropes chosen to give your readers the frights they seek. Each prompt is divided into several sections to help you clarify plot points, deepen your characters, detail their emotional journeys, create conflict, and develop new scenes. At the end of each chapter, you'll find a series of Quick Writes prompts that are meant to be done fast, like a lightning round in a game show where the loser dies. Don't overthink—just write.

Do these prompts at the beginning of a writing session to get yourself into a creative flow. Remember that the specific details in each prompt are meant as suggestions. If some parts of a prompt apply to the story you're writing but other parts don't, feel free to adjust as necessary. The intention is to get you thinking, exploring, and writing.

These prompts are fuel for your creative engine. Let your imagination run wild as you dive into the exercises in this book. Unleash your passion for scary stories and let the words flow. It's time for you to delve into depravity and dread as you bring your horror novel to life.

I KNOW WHAT YOU DID

Once upon a time, your protagonist did something bad. Not just bad but illegal, unethical, even sinful. She tried to bury it in the past. (There may have even been a literal burial in the woods under cover of night.) But the frustrating truth about secrets is it's nearly impossible to keep them forever. Because if someone else knows, someone else can tell. And her whole world is about to be turned upside when someone tells her: I Know What You Did.

This mistake from her past haunts her. But this person (or creature, or entity) who *knows* about it will haunt her even more. He wants revenge. And he won't stop slashing anyone and anything in his way until he gets to your protagonist. Let the bloodbath begin!

How will your protagonist respond? She would do anything to keep from being exposed, so what happens when she feels cornered? How many more bad decisions can she make? Might she commit the same sin again, or do something even worse?

One thing to consider: It's possible she didn't do her terrible deed alone. What if her friends were involved too? Does that mean they're all being stalked? Could the threats be coming from within their group? How do you get out of trouble when there's no one you can trust, or when the only people you can ask for help might be the ones who want you dead? Keep turning the screws until the very end of your story.

There's Blood on Your Shirt 

SCENARIO

Your protagonist wakes up disoriented. He isn't quite sure where he is or how he got here. He has a raging headache, which is strange because he doesn't remember drinking. He's about to call a friend for help when he notices: There's a dead body in the room.

BRAINSTORM

Map out the sequence of events that led to this moment. Figure out everything your protagonist doesn't remember. Does he know the victim? Did he kill this person? If not, who did, and how did they do it? Come up with at least three actions or choices your protagonist made during those blackout hours that he'll regret when he ultimately pieces together what really happened.

WRITE

Think about how your protagonist disposes of the body. What type of person is he? Is this something that comes naturally? Is he good at problem-solving? Is he physically fit or more of an intellectual? Is it daytime, or can he hide in the shadows? Is it hot out, or does he have to deal with snow or rain? Now write a scene that comes after the body disposal where he encounters someone (either a friend or a stranger) who confronts him about an obvious bloodstain on his clothes.

Remember: There's someone out there who knows what happened while your protagonist was blacked out. Someone who could provide answers. But what if this other character holds the key to your protagonist's guilt? Could he live with himself if he knows he's capable of such brutality?

OPTIONAL ELEMENTS TO INCLUDE

- A mysterious bruise on your protagonist's neck.
- A wad of cash.
- The bloody murder weapon is in his pocket.

Horror Twist

What if someone spies on your protagonist while he disposes of the body? An unknown figure lurks in the shadows, keeps tabs on his every move, and then follows him home.

Callbacks

Deep down, your protagonist knows the truth. Find a moment where he briefly remembers a moment right before the victim's death, but the memory doesn't make sense to him yet. Or maybe the gruesome memory implicates him in the murder. Does your protagonist tell anyone, or does he do something drastic to himself to suppress the memory?

I Wouldn't Go If I Were You

SCENARIO

Your protagonist receives a mysterious message inviting him back to his hometown. It's more of a summons than a request, and there's also something ominous about the note: an implication or a pointed jab. He swore he'd never go back there—because that's where his long-concealed bloody crime took place. It would be insanity to go back now, right?

BRAINSTORM

What did your protagonist do? How long has he kept it hidden? Who else knows about it? Who might your protagonist be trying to protect?

WRITE

Write a scene where your protagonist asks a trusted friend for advice. He knows it isn't wise to return home, but he's worried about who might get hurt if he doesn't go.

Remember: Think about the dangers that await your protagonist the second he returns to this place he's forsaken.

OPTIONAL ELEMENTS TO INCLUDE

- A bad omen.
- A warning from a stranger.
- An animal carcass.

Horror Twist

Home can be a place of unprocessed trauma for your protagonist. It makes him feel like a different person. What if your protagonist has dissociative identity disorder? His alter egos haven't appeared in years, but when he returns home, he can't control who comes out to play.

“If You Wanted to Kill Me, You Would’ve Done It Already”

SCENARIO

Sleepless nights. Panic when the phone rings. That heavy feeling in the pit of her stomach every time she turns a corner. Your protagonist doesn’t feel safe anywhere. A stranger has been stalking her, following her, chasing her. No matter where she is, no matter what she’s doing, she can’t shake the feeling that she’s being watched. And then the inexplicable happens: She’s taken.

BRAINSTORM

Your protagonist’s stalker is motivated by revenge. He knows about a crime she committed, and he won’t let her get away with it. Think about what goes through your protagonist’s head before she learns his motivations. Does she have a guilty conscience? Does she think about her past crime constantly, or has she buried it so deep that it doesn’t weigh on her anymore?

WRITE

Write a monologue for your protagonist where she tries to reason with her stalker/kidnapper. She begs him to let her go. Maybe she tries to make him see her as a person he can empathize with. Have her try several different tactics as her desperation grows.

Remember: Even if your protagonist has tried to sublimate her feelings of guilt, a part of her has always known the past would come back to haunt her. Part of her thinks she deserves this. How can you make the antagonist’s attempt to punish her feel both surprising and inevitable?

OPTIONAL ELEMENTS TO INCLUDE

- A rabid animal.
- A string of obscenities shouted angrily.
- An earnest plea for forgiveness.

Horror Twist

Add a terrifying ticking clock to the scene. If your protagonist doesn't say what her captor wants to hear before a specific time, he will hurt someone she loves. There's no turning back after that. But she doesn't know what he wants to hear, so she's scrambling for the right words.

Callbacks

Her kidnapper has been watching her for a while. He hates to see her living a normal life that seems to be guilt-free when her actions took so much from him. When did he decide to stop watching her and take her fate into his own hands? Did something specific trigger his escalation?

Quick Writes

Set a timer for 15 minutes and do not stop writing until the timer goes off. Do not edit, cross out, or censor yourself. Write down every thought that comes to you.

1. Your protagonist discovers a handwritten threat. The message alludes to something bad he thought he got away with. Write a scene where he desperately tries to destroy the message before anyone else sees it.
2. Write a scene where your protagonist buries a body but accidentally leaves behind something that could identify her. (Anything from an item of jewelry to her wallet to her cell phone.) By the time she realizes her mistake, it's too late.
3. One of your protagonist's loved ones has been possessed by a demon, ghost, or other evil entity. Write a scene where the possessed loved one confronts your protagonist about a literal skeleton in his closet.
4. Write a scene where your protagonist confesses to an act of manslaughter that he thinks he got away with. He doesn't realize it, but someone is listening, and the listener uses the overheard confession to coerce him into committing another murder.
5. When she was young, your protagonist killed a friend. Write a scene where someone confronts her about it, so she kills them too. Unfortunately, they told someone else they were going to confront her. Who else knows? How many people will she have to kill?

STRANGER DANGER

How do you know you weren't followed home by a psychopath? That stranger at the coffee shop who smiled at you, who you later saw again in the parking lot—you want to believe that was a coincidence. But what if he was taking note of the car you drive so he can hide in the back seat later and strangle you from behind?

Now imagine you're alone in a subway car when a strange man sits across from you and won't stop staring. When you get off at your stop, he follows you. If you walk home, he'll know where you live. Suddenly your fears go into overdrive. Are you overreacting or should you get help?

Or imagine someone from the Department of Water and Power comes over to check one of your meters. When you let him in, you get a bad feeling in your gut: How do you know this person is really who he says he is? What if this stranger you just *invited into your home* wants to slice you up and take a piece of you with him as a perverse trophy? What the hell do you do?

When it comes to encounters with creepy strangers, the psychological terror of what *could* happen is sometimes just as scary as what does happen. But your characters would be wise to follow their instincts when they sense Stranger Danger. It's possible their worst nightmares are about to come true.

"Get As Far from Him As You Can"

SCENARIO

There's a chase. A killer hunting his prey. When he finally attacks, it's brutal. He leaves his victim for dead, but they aren't. Not quite. Not yet. And that's when your protagonist enters the scene. She has no idea there's a murderous lunatic on the loose; she's just focused on saving this stranger's life.

BRAINSTORM

This hasn't been a great day for your protagonist, and things are about to get a whole lot worse. Think about everything on her mind before she encounters this dying person. What's weighing her down? Put her at a crossroads in both her personal and professional life. Really clarify what she's going through immediately before the start of this scene to give yourself a sense of what her emotional headspace is like.

WRITE

Write a scene where your protagonist stumbles upon a person who's just been attacked, and she launches into action to help. Maybe the person can't speak at first because they're too badly injured. But at some point, they warn your protagonist that the attacker is nearby, watching: "He'll come for you next." Your protagonist has no idea what the attacker looks like. He could be anyone.

OPTIONAL ELEMENTS TO INCLUDE

- A bloody footprint.
- An everyday item used as a weapon.
- A scream in the distance—someone else has been attacked.

Horror Twist

The killer doesn't have to be human. How would this scene change if he were a vampire, a werewolf, or a demon? Who knows how many evil creatures might be lurking in the shadows?

Callbacks

Does the attacker accidentally leave anything behind that would give away his identity? If so, what might this object be? Think of it as a bread crumb that will send your protagonist on an unexpected journey. But is she pursuing this deadly stranger, or is he pursuing her?

“Mind If I Use Your Phone?”

SCENARIO

Your protagonist is running errands. Maybe he's filling up his gas tank or getting groceries. He doesn't think much of it when a friendly stranger says her phone is dead and asks if she can use his for a quick call. He will regret this good deed forever.

BRAINSTORM

Think about how much you can learn about a person from their cell phone. Scroll through yours right now, skim through the apps, open your photos, and glance at your notes. How much of your life could a stranger steal in 60 seconds?

WRITE

Write a sequence of scenes where your protagonist realizes how much this stranger learned about him from his phone. Maybe she wasn't as friendly as she seemed?

OPTIONAL ELEMENTS TO INCLUDE

- She brushes her hand against his.
- He notices an unusual smell.
- He tells her a lie that she will call him out on later.

Horror Twist

Is her phone really dead? What if it isn't even her phone? She could have stolen it from the last guy she killed. It would only take her a few seconds to share your protagonist's location with herself so she can follow his every move.

"You Should've Locked Your Door"

SCENARIO

A killer's on the loose. Your protagonist just got home from work and wants to relax. Maybe she'll take a bath, drink some wine, or curl up on the couch with a book. Unfortunately, she won't get the peace and quiet she craves, because she isn't as alone as she thinks she is.

BRAINSTORM

Your protagonist is in mourning. Her whole life was recently shattered by the death of a close confidant, and she feels completely alone. In what ways does her grief manifest? Think of it as something omnipresent that she carries with her like a heavy blanket. What was the worst part of her day, and how was it colored by her emotional turmoil? Of course, the tragic irony is that her day is about to get much, much worse.

WRITE

Write a scene where a dangerous killer/monster/demon enters your protagonist's haven. Let your readers in on the fact that someone (or something) else is there before your protagonist discovers she isn't alone. Draw out that tension as long as you can. Let her get several steps into her self-care routine before she knows she's in danger. Then, build to a confrontation between your protagonist and the intruder.

Remember: If one more bad thing happens to your protagonist, she just might snap. Think about how you can use her frayed nerves to take this scene in an unexpected direction.

OPTIONAL ELEMENTS TO INCLUDE

- An overhead light goes out.
- The power dynamics shift.
- Your protagonist gets distracted by a phone call.

Horror Twist

This could be a scene with a supporting character whose luck has run out. Instead of getting away with their life, they become another victim. Think about whose death would have a great impact on your protagonist, then lure your protagonist into the killer's vicinity to witness the murder.

Callbacks

A stranger penetrating the safe confines of a person's home is scary. But your readers will be thrown even more off balance if you introduce the killer before the intrusion and show what he's capable of. If your readers already know how bloodthirsty he is at the top of your scene, you'll be able to layer in even more tension and terror when he's invading your protagonist's private space.

Quick Writes

Set a timer for 15 minutes and do not stop writing until the timer goes off. Do not edit, cross out, or censor yourself. Write down every thought that comes to you.

1. Write a scene where your protagonist sets out on a road trip, but doesn't realize a psychotic stranger is hiding in the back seat. He has a rope.
2. Your protagonist thinks he's doing a good deed by helping a stranger (perhaps buying them a meal), and then the stranger takes advantage of his kindness. Write a scene where at least two fingers are severed.
3. Your protagonist gets trapped with a stranger in a confined space (maybe a stalled subway car or a busted elevator). Write a scene where he realizes his companion is a dangerous maniac.
4. Write a scene where your protagonist accidentally cuts off a stranger in traffic and the stranger angrily pursues him. Think of it as the worst case of road rage in history.
5. Your protagonist works in retail and deals with hundreds of strangers every day. Write a scene where he receives an angry message from a customer threatening to hurt him. But he has no idea who wants him dead.

RITUAL KILLINGS

You think serial killers are scary? They work alone. A group of people who kill together is far more terrifying. Especially a group that kills to make a peace offering to a vengeful god or a supernatural deity. The people who participate in ritual killing are like serial killers in overdrive.

Your protagonist might encounter human sacrifice from many angles. Maybe he joins a cult and learns that a tradition of ritual killing has been established to maintain a sense of order within the cult's caste system. Or maybe she's a cop who goes undercover to investigate an unusual string of murders, and she encounters a group of people who think they're holding the fabric of society together through their ritualistic, murderous acts. Or perhaps he was nearly a victim of a ritual killing, and he's haunted by the fear that his former captors might find him again.

As they say, the devil is in the details—literally, in this case. So, when you're writing a Ritual Killing horror story, don't forget about the *ritual* aspect. Think about how much planning your characters do before they kill. Have fun with these details, and make sure they're unique. The more specific your Ritual Killings are, the more real they're going to feel to your readers. Try to make their skin crawl!

Wash Away My Sins

SCENARIO

In his former life as an undercover cop, your protagonist witnessed a ritual killing. Ever since then, he's been wracked with guilt over not doing more to stop it. Doing so would have exposed his identity and put him in danger, but he still feels immense shame over his inaction.

BRAINSTORM

What did the ritual look, feel, sound, and smell like? Describe it using vivid, emotional imagery. Then get into your protagonist's head in that pivotal moment: Write his stream of thoughts as he watched an innocent person die. Let those thoughts be chaotic. Think of this as a moment that changed his brain chemistry. His life can now be divided into the "before" and the "after." There's no going back to a more innocent time after seeing such savagery firsthand.

WRITE

Write a scene where your protagonist obsessively washes his body to feel cleansed of his emotionally grimy past, but it doesn't work. Take him through a series of ablution rituals that get more extreme as they progress. Lean into the realm of body horror as he attempts to mutilate his memories by literally purifying his physical form.

OPTIONAL ELEMENTS TO INCLUDE

- Chanting in another language.
- An electrical hum.
- The scraping of skin.

Horror Twist

Your protagonist may think he's escaped his past, but his past isn't done with him. What if members of the cult he once infiltrated are secretly stalking him? There's no way they're going to let him escape. Once you're "family," that's forever. Turns out he has more to fear than just his demons from the past. The people he once knew are still as present as ever—he just doesn't know it yet.

Callbacks

Your protagonist is haunted by the ritual killing he witnessed. Play around with the idea that he has tried to shut out the memories but specific details keep coming back to him. Think of it as a haunting that keeps taking place inside his head. Memories tend to distort with time; what if his memories keep getting more vivid and violent?

You Are the Necessary Sacrifice

SCENARIO

Your cult-loving protagonist spends the day preparing for a sacrifice. She makes sure her group has everything the ceremony requires, tends to the needs of her elders, and ensures that the stage has been set for a successful ritual. But she doesn't yet know who tonight's victim will be.

BRAINSTORM

Think about what your protagonist is running away from. In what ways did her loved ones fail her? Why did she seek out the found family of this cult? Does she think she's finally found the life she's looking for? Explore all the reasons she feels safe here.

WRITE

Write a scene where your protagonist discovers she's been helping prepare for her own sacrifice. Only now does she realize she doesn't want to die. Can she change her elders' minds, or must she attempt an escape?

OPTIONAL ELEMENTS TO INCLUDE

- Her closest ally unexpectedly turns on her.
- A goblet filled with blood.
- A locked door.

Horror Twist

What are the core tenets of this cult? Come up with a list of beliefs that incorporates ideas from multiple religions—but find ways to twist them toward evil. Think about how the cult leaders benefit from the death of innocent members.

Look in My Eyes

SCENARIO

Your protagonist is caught in a time loop. He was murdered in a ritual killing, and now he keeps reliving his death. The worst moment of his life happens again and again and again. Is there any way he can change his fate? Or is he destined to keep dying the same grisly death forever?

BRAINSTORM

Time loop stories require precision. Sketch out all the actions that take place leading up to the ritual killing of your protagonist. Then make several lists of alternate outcomes that could occur with slight changes in these actions.

WRITE

Write a scene where your protagonist tries to connect with his killer. Perhaps he makes an appeal for another chance. Or he tries to get his killer to see him as human. Write the scene five times, with five wildly different outcomes. Push the scares further with each successive version of the scene.

Remember: Repetition is a feature of many rituals. Can you find a way to incorporate the idea of the time loop into the ritual itself? Think about how the rules of the time loop and the rules of the ritual killing might coincide.

OPTIONAL ELEMENTS TO INCLUDE

- An act of disrobing.
- A plea to God.
- A chill in the air.

Horror Twist

What if your protagonist, unbeknownst to himself, is the bad guy? You're telling the story from his point of view, and he sees himself as the hero of his own story. But consider the idea that he was chosen for this ritual killing because of monstrous deeds he has inflicted upon the world.

Callbacks

Each version of the ritual killing should escalate the stakes and tension for your protagonist. Think about the signs your protagonist might see that would indicate he's broken out of the loop. Aside from his survival, are there any other clues you can weave into the story that tell your readers the loop has finally been closed?

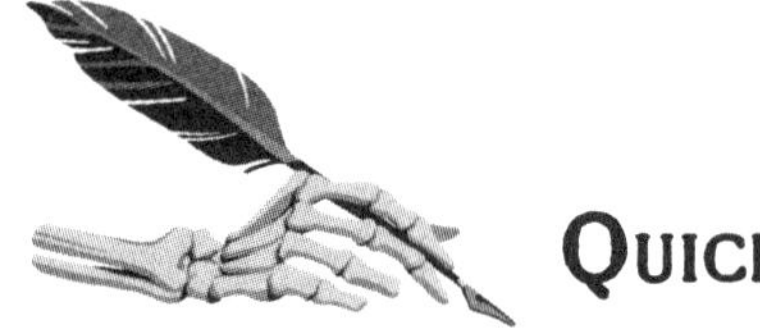

Quick Writes

Set a timer for 15 minutes and do not stop writing until the timer goes off. Do not edit, cross out, or censor yourself. Write down every thought that comes to you.

1. Write a scene where a coven of witches performs a ritual sacrifice, draining the essence of one of your protagonist's loved ones to attain youth, beauty, wealth, or a sinful pleasure.
2. Your protagonist infiltrates a cult to save a loved one. Write a scene where she is asked to play a role in a ritual sacrifice to prove her loyalty to the group.
3. Write a scene where your protagonist discovers a death mask and investigates its ritual sacrifice origins. Why does he feel like the mask is calling to him and compelling him to use it?
4. Your protagonist discovers her parents have joined a multi-level marketing scheme and are planning to sacrifice her to prove that they have no ties to the outside world. Write a scene where your protagonist must fight off her parents.
5. Your protagonist broke free from a social group that secretly practiced Satanism and performed ritual sacrifices. Write a scene where a member of the group blackmails him to bring him back into the fold.

SEX KILLS

When a supporting character loses his virginity, or when a couple clearly enjoys getting it on, readers know: *Oh, they're about to die.* There's a reason "body count" refers to both how many people a murderer has killed and how many people a selfish lover has bedded. One of the most enduring horror tropes is the use of sex to foreshadow death. In horror stories, Sex Kills.

But why? You might argue that this is a conservative trope carried over from more puritan times—until you really think about the purpose of literary sex. These scenes let readers in on a moment where your characters have completely let their guard down, where they're fully trusting each other. Which puts them in a place of vulnerability. In turn, this makes it harder for them to survive whatever horrors are coming their way. If a character wants to live to see the rest of the book series, they must be aware of their surroundings; they must put up protective walls, both metaphorically and literally. Vulnerability is great for sex, but not for surviving the grim reaper!

You can also have fun subverting this trope. Kill the character who's saving himself for marriage and let your most promiscuous character be the Final Girl. Keep your readers guessing.

“This Is the Best Night of My Life”

SCENARIO

Dating is full of highs and lows. You might find the love of your life (high), or you might get murdered (low). But your protagonist has a good feeling about tonight's date. Unfortunately, so does your antagonist, but for very different reasons. One will have the best night of their life; the other is about to die.

BRAINSTORM

Think through two parallel scenes. Two people (of any gender) are getting ready for a date. One goes through the traditional beats of a pre-date routine. They take a shower, go through various beauty rituals, agonize over outfit choices, and so on. The other goes through a more murderous pre-date routine: It still might include a shower, beauty rituals, and outfit debates, but it also includes things like knife sharpening and online stalking.

WRITE

Write a date scene where your protagonist is completely clueless about their date's murderous intentions. Don't make your protagonist dumb; it's more that their menacing date is extremely good at hiding who they really are. Play around with point of view. Get into both characters' heads as the date barrels toward a bedroom finish. Tease out the tension so your readers are screaming at your protagonist to get out before it's too late.

OPTIONAL ELEMENTS TO INCLUDE

- A slow striptease.
- A photo taken surreptitiously.
- They bond over their mutually terrible childhoods.

Horror Twist

The date leaves your protagonist for dead. But as soon as they're gone, your protagonist opens their eyes. They need help, and fast. Every cell in their body hurts as they desperately try to crawl across the room to their phone. If they survive tonight, they are going to relive every single moment of this date, looking for all the red flags they missed.

Callbacks

Look at the opening and closing moments of their date. Can you plant anything in the opening image that foreshadows the horrors to come? Think about how much your protagonist changes from the first moment of this date to the last.

Do You Regret It Now?

SCENARIO

An unknown figure moves through a crowd. Maybe the gathering is a music festival, Burning Man, a frat party, or an outdoor wedding reception. The unknown figure spies two people hooking up in a dark place on the fringes of the crowd. The figure watches. Waiting. Judging. Ready to kill.

BRAINSTORM

Get inside the killer's head. What do they find triggering about sex? Have unresolved traumas from their past damaged them in some way?

WRITE

Write a scene from the perspective of one of the two people hooking up. They didn't want to do it here, because they felt too exposed, but they let their urges get the better of them. When the sexual encounter ends, these two characters go their separate ways—and the unknown figure follows your protagonist.

OPTIONAL ELEMENTS TO INCLUDE

- A ripped item of clothing.
- The sound of someone else's heavy breathing.
- An unused condom repurposed as a weapon.

Horror Twist

The killer doesn't have to be human. They could be a monster, an alien, a ghost, or something else. Regardless, they're disgusted by the behavior they witness; they're going to make these fornicators pay for their promiscuity.

You Should've Swiped Left

SCENARIO

Your protagonist meets a guy on one of the apps. They go on a fun and unique date; she's impressed by how thoughtful he was about planning a night he knew she would like, based on what he learned about her from her profile. They end up back at his place, where they hook up. The sex is great, and this guy checks all her boxes. Too bad he's a killer.

BRAINSTORM

Open a dating app and look at the various prompts they give you when creating a profile. Answer all these questions in the voice of your protagonist. Then imagine how the killer might plan the perfect night using the information your protagonist has provided him. Does she share anything seemingly innocuous that, in hindsight, might expose too much personal information?

WRITE

Write a post-sex scene where your protagonist discovers her date isn't who he said he is. She's inside his home, and it slowly dawns on her that she's trapped here. What does she do to try to escape? Build to a moment where she does something drastic to break free and it backfires on her. Now she's really trapped, and she's made him angry. Don't poke the bear.

Remember: Your protagonist has probably been on a lot of bad dates, but this is easily the worst. Think about what you want to say about how difficult it is to find love. If dating is like a horror story, what's the scariest thing about it?

OPTIONAL ELEMENTS TO INCLUDE

- She scrolls through his phone and finds something disturbing.
- Handcuffs.
- She hears another voice in the house.

Horror Twist

Build to a moment where your protagonist discovers someone else who's also trapped in the house, chained to a bed or a water heater in a hidden room. They help each other escape, but then this accomplice turns out to be even more of a monster than the first bad guy.

Quick Writes

Set a timer for 15 minutes and do not stop writing until the timer goes off. Do not edit, cross out, or censor yourself. Write down every thought that comes to you.

1. Write a scene where your protagonist takes a post-sex shower and is completely oblivious as her lover is murdered in the bedroom.
2. Your protagonist has new neighbors in his apartment building, and everyone can hear them having sex. Write a scene where the neighbors suddenly stop making noises and your protagonist is grateful for the quiet. He has no idea the silence will be permanent.
3. Write a scene where your protagonist uses her sexual prowess to lure a monster into her arms and then sucks out his life essence. Interpret this as you'd like, but by the time she's through with him, he's dead.
4. Write a scene where your protagonist goes on a blind date. A voice in his head tells him to end the date early: *If you do, you'll live; if you don't, you'll die.* He listens to his gut, but now his date is following him.
5. Your antagonist is afraid of sex. Do a deep dive into her backstory and come up with a reason the act of sex is such a trigger. Write a scene where this fear transforms her into a monster.

UNSEEN MONSTER

How do you fight off an evil that literally can't be seen? You don't dare let down your guard, because you know your enemy is out there somewhere—and you know it's coming for you. It's in the air somehow, like an infectious virus that can hurt you even though you never lay eyes on it. An Unseen Monster can inflict more damage on the psyche than any physical blow.

It can overwhelm you; it can take control; it can drive you to the brink of despair and make you do things you never in your right mind thought you could ever do. It feeds on your fears. It creates a feeling of existential dread in the pit of your stomach. You worry you'll never feel normal again. There will always be a part of you that wonders, *Is it still out there, coming for me?* It will get under your skin and never leave.

Just because the monster is unseen at first doesn't mean it won't ever show itself. You might build to a visual reveal later in your story, a moment when the monster finally appears in corporeal form. But if you let your protagonist (and your readers) see it, make sure the monster's as scary as they imagined.

Show Your Face

SCENARIO

Your protagonist is dealing with an inordinate amount of stress. Maybe he's going through a divorce. His kid could be acting out and getting into trouble at school. He can barely afford the terrible apartment he just moved into, even though it's falling apart. Everything that could go wrong is going wrong. And that's when he starts hearing the voices.

BRAINSTORM

Quickly brainstorm what your protagonist's best day ever looked like. Paint a clear picture of one of his highest highs as a counterpoint to this lowest of lows he's in now. How much has he lost?

WRITE

Write a scene where your protagonist has a conversation with a voice only he can hear—a voice that's urging him to commit a bad deed. Your protagonist wants the voice to show itself. There must be an entity of some sort—perhaps an alien or a demon—who's hijacked his head. If the voice really wants him to do this heinous thing, it must show itself! Come out of hiding, voice!

Remember: You decide if your protagonist is having a psychotic break or the voice belongs to an external antagonist. Either way, let the voice push him to a breaking point. What happens when your protagonist does this bad thing he doesn't want to do? How will he justify his actions if he ever realizes that *he* is the unseen monster?

OPTIONAL ELEMENTS TO INCLUDE

- An act of cutting.
- A creature crawls out of your protagonist's mouth.
- He is consumed by shadows.

Horror Twist

What if the voice is trying to help him seek revenge? The target might be anyone from the ex who doesn't love him anymore to the boss who doesn't appreciate him to his ungrateful kid who won't stop acting out. (Hurting the kid would be terrible, but he keeps telling himself these aren't *his* thoughts and feelings—they're the voice's.)

Callbacks

Go back to that "best day" you brainstormed. Are there any sounds, scents, feelings, images, words, or sensations that might bring the memories of this day back for your protagonist? Is it possible to remind him who he used to be, or is that guy gone?

I Can Hear You Breathing

SCENARIO

While helping clean out a loved one's basement (or perhaps a long-forgotten storage closet at work), your protagonist accidentally unleashes an ancient evil spirit that can enter a person's body and control their actions. It leaps from one body to the next as it causes chaos and goes on a murderous spree. Your protagonist feels guilty about opening this proverbial Pandora's box; he's determined to trap it again and end the bloody rampage.

BRAINSTORM

What's the origin story of this evil spirit? Why does it have such a hunger for blood? What are its weaknesses? How did it get trapped in this basement in the first place? What would your protagonist have to do to capture it? (You might not want to answer all these questions in your story, but it'll be helpful for you to know the answers as you write.)

WRITE

Your protagonist stalks this evil entity, tracking its whereabouts, studying how it moves, trying to determine how, when, and why it leaves one person to inhabit another. He believes if he can figure out what drives the entity's behavior, he can conquer it. Write a scene where he meets someone who survived an encounter with the evil spirit; have that character reveal what it felt like to have this entity controlling his body. As they talk, the survivor can sense that the entity is nearby.

OPTIONAL ELEMENTS TO INCLUDE

- A terrible confession.
- A deep physical scar.
- Your protagonist must quickly flee.

Horror Twist

When the entity controls someone, there are slight changes in their appearance. Think of one or two visual cues your protagonist might pick up on—things he could look for in every person he encounters to determine whether he's safe with them or not.

Callbacks

Your protagonist set this evil loose. Maybe defeating the entity requires a trip back to the place where that happened. There might be a clue that your protagonist missed.

“Promise You Won’t Open the Door, No Matter What”

SCENARIO

Your protagonist has several kids she’s trying to protect from a demon or ghost living in their home. It’s almost like the house itself is possessed. Even though this demon can’t be seen, it has a powerful presence. Your protagonist feels it in the air, in the furniture, in the walls. So do her kids. She’s determined to reclaim their home.

BRAINSTORM

Think about how a child might be affected by a ghost or a demon. Can young children see the unseen? What might your protagonist learn from her children about her home’s evil inhabitant?

WRITE

Write a scene where your protagonist has a physical altercation with this unseen monster while her kids listen from the other room. You might build to a moment where one of her children breaks into the room to help her, but instead they put your protagonist in greater danger.

OPTIONAL ELEMENTS TO INCLUDE

- Furniture that bleeds.
- Someone is consumed by (or sucked into) a wall.
- The house sinks.

Horror Twist

The last thing a parent wants to do is hurt their child. What would your protagonist do if the Unseen Monster took possession of her kid? Could she lure it out and get her child to safety?

Quick Writes

Set a timer for 15 minutes and do not stop writing until the timer goes off. Do not edit, cross out, or censor yourself. Write down every thought that comes to you.

1. Your protagonist befriends a murderous chatbot. The closer they get, the more delusional your protagonist is: He believes his friend is real. Write a scene where the chatbot convinces your protagonist to commit a murder in its name.
2. There is a monster so terrifying that people are literally scared to death when they look at it. Write a scene where your protagonist blinds himself to escape this fate.
3. Your protagonist is on the hunt for a new home. Write a scene where he falls in love with a house that just went on the market but a stranger warns him, "Evil lives here."
4. Your protagonist is a great horror writer, but her words come true as she writes them. Write a scene where she brainstorms ideas about a horrific murder, unleashing an Unseen Monster that is about to turn on her.
5. Your protagonist shares a secret with a trusted friend: One of her parents was haunted by an Unseen Monster, and she's afraid the monster is after her now. What does this monster represent thematically?

HAUNTED HOUSE

Your home is supposed to be your safe space—a sanctuary where you are free of everything that scares you in the outside world. When you're at home, you're in charge. You can lock your door and shut out all the bad stuff.

But what if you can't? What if the things you fear most are *inside* your home? What if they're living in your walls, moving through your air vents, or manifesting themselves in all the cozy spots where you used to find comfort? What if they're hiding in the nooks and crannies of your house, giving every shadow a sinister edge? Suddenly this place you once loved is the last place you want to be. This is why Haunted House stories speak to our most primal fears.

When writing a Haunted House story, you'll want to explore how the house became haunted. Maybe it was built on an ancient burial ground, and your characters are being terrorized by spirits who lost their last resting place. Maybe one of your characters accidentally summons demons in a meditation ceremony gone awry. Maybe one of the previous tenants died here and won't leave. Or maybe there's no explanation at all, which might be even scarier than knowing who or what is haunting you.

“It Comes Alive at Night”

SCENARIO

Your characters have just moved into a new home, but based on the sounds they hear at night, they suspect its previous occupants never left—not exactly, at least. As soon as night falls, the spirits come out to play.

BRAINSTORM

Think about the spirits who live here. How do they feel about human strangers sharing their space, and what behavior makes them mad? Do some brainstorming about how they've interacted with guests in the past, and how their previous haunts have primed them for this one.

WRITE

One of your characters wakes up in the middle of the night to grab a midnight snack. Write a scene where they're still in their groggy half-awake state and an appliance or piece of furniture attacks them. This scene might be funny before your character realizes what's going on. The house is alive!

OPTIONAL ELEMENTS TO INCLUDE

- A sharp kitchen object hovering in the air.
- A strangled scream.
- Poison.

Horror Twist

How many people have died in this house? What if each successive death makes the house more powerful? The longer you stay here, the more likely you are to die. Perhaps one of the house's previous guests takes corporeal form to deliver a warning, but it goes unheeded.

Whatever You Do, Never Go Into the Attic

SCENARIO

Your protagonist is staying at a vacation home with his family for the summer. When the family sees the house for the first time, they are explicitly told to stay out of the attic. As soon as they learn it is off limits, everyone becomes curious. What is it about human nature that makes people always want to do things they've been told they can't do?

BRAINSTORM

Write several short scenes where members of the family consider exploring the attic—or they almost go up there, then change their mind at the last moment. Explore how the attic seems to be calling to them. Do they hear sounds? Make a list of at least ten things they might be horrified to discover within the confines of that forbidden room.

WRITE

Write a scene where one of your characters goes into the attic alone. Whatever they discover up there, it changes them. Some possibilities: They see something so terrifying that they never speak again; they are possessed by an ancient spirit who has lived in this house for decades; or they meet a twisted doppelgänger who steals their soul.

Remember: Just because one character didn't heed the warning and faced immediate consequences, that doesn't mean your other characters will lose their curiosity. The attic is calling to them, and they all want to answer. Think of this as a morality tale about how sometimes people need to learn the same lesson repeatedly before it finally sinks in.

OPTIONAL ELEMENTS TO INCLUDE

- A bloodless body.
- A gust of wind inside the house.
- The walls bend and break.

Horror Twist

This is a summer vacation to remember, but for all the wrong reasons. What if your protagonist knew this house was haunted when he booked the rental? He doesn't believe in ghosts, so he just thought it would make for a good story later. Now he wishes he could take all this back.

"I Felt Her Touch Me"

SCENARIO

Your protagonist suspects her house is haunted. She's lived here with her husband and children for years, and she's always had a strange feeling that something about the house was *off*. So, she hires a medium to cleanse the home of any spirits who might be hanging around. She does this against the better judgment of the rest of her family (they either think it's a dumb idea, or they're scared of what might happen).

BRAINSTORM

How long has your protagonist lived here? Come up with at least five specific moments when she thought she could feel another presence with her. Describe the presence from her perspective with as much detail as you can.

WRITE

Write a scene where a medium performs a ceremony to exorcise spirits from your protagonist's home. Instead of banishing them, though, the medium inadvertently brings a ghost (or several) closer to the surface of human perception. In doing so, she gives this ghost (or ghosts) power. Lots of power. Your protagonist never should have gone down this road. Her life is about to become a living hell.

Remember: Your protagonist's family might not believe in ghosts, and perhaps they think the medium is a con artist. What's the moment when they all realize that Mom is right?

OPTIONAL ELEMENTS TO INCLUDE

- Indentations on your protagonist's skin.
- A sudden chill in the air.
- A household object explodes.

Horror Twist

Your protagonist is a believer. Where did these convictions come from? Maybe she once, long ago, had a terrifying encounter with a ghost. She's never been able to shake it. In fact, maybe it isn't her house that's haunted—it's her. This ghost has been following her around—it's attached itself to her—and now she's given it power.

Callbacks

This ghost has a deep connection to your protagonist. What if the ghost can summon her worst fears and memories, digging deep into her subconscious and pulling up all the fears that she most wishes she could bury?

Quick Writes

Set a timer for 15 minutes and do not stop writing until the timer goes off. Do not edit, cross out, or censor yourself. Write down every thought that comes to you.

1. To receive his inheritance, your protagonist must spend 24 hours in a haunted house. Write a scene where he encounters an angry apparition who doesn't want him to succeed.
2. Write a scene where your protagonist gets trapped inside a small space in his home (anything from a closet to the oven to a crawlspace) as a malevolent spirit tries to attack him.
3. Your protagonist learns that the previous owner of her home was murdered in the dining room. Write a scene where she has a brief run-in with the owner's ghost, who mistakenly believes she's the murderer.
4. Write a scene where your protagonist senses a spectral being in his bedroom. The shadowy figure is closer than he realizes. (Maybe it's even inside him, somehow?) It wants to consume your protagonist's hopes, dreams, and desires.
5. Write a scene where your protagonist performs a complicated ritual to expel several angry spirits from her home. Think about how she learned about this ritual and what it might entail. Something goes wrong, and she infects herself with the spirits' anger.

HIDDEN PASSAGES

Sometimes terror lies just below the surface—literally, in the case of Hidden Passages. Imagine you're sleeping in your bed at night, safe and sound, when your closet door slowly opens. A skittish man with a gaunt face, mangy hair, and dirty fingernails crawls out of the darkness, ready to explore. Oddly, he appears to have emerged out of a secret door inside your closet. It leads down to a dark and dingy shelter under your house: a room you never knew existed. Awful things happen down there. Things you don't want to know about. Unfortunately, when you find that secret passage, there's no turning back.

When you were a kid, your parents probably told you not to worry about monsters under your bed. But what did they know? Well, they were right about one thing, at least. The monsters aren't directly under your bed; they're below the floorboards too—in the secret dungeon, or the hidden torture room, or the makeshift kill room. When those monsters finally get you, it'll be too late to tell your parents "I told you so." But you'll know in your heart how deadly wrong they were.

The thing about Hidden Passages is they can be anywhere. You never know what creatures, monsters, and evil entities might be lurking nearby where you can't see them.

"I Don't Think We Should Go Down There"

SCENARIO

Your characters are up to some mischief: They're exploring an abandoned building, or they're sneaking into a friend's home, or they're breaking into the mall after hours. They find a hidden door; behind it is a stairway that descends into shadows. Someone suggests seeing what's down there, but others aren't so sure that's a good idea. They shouldn't even be here! It would probably be smarter to go home. But they've come this far, haven't they? Why not explore a little more?

BRAINSTORM

Make a list of at least twenty terrible things they might discover at the bottom of those stairs. Let each of your ideas be more twisted, grotesque, and disturbing than the last. When you've come up with the most upsetting image possible, go darker. (You can always pull back later, so give yourself permission to push things to the extreme.) What would make your characters wish they never came down here to investigate?

WRITE

Write a scene where your protagonists descend the stairs despite their apprehensions. As soon as they reach the bottom, they encounter a violent monster. Let the scene ramp up to a state of chaos. At least one person dies, one is taken away to an unknown location, and one is injured.

Remember: Any monster might be waiting for them at the bottom of those stairs. Let your imagination go wild. Come up with something your readers have never seen before.

OPTIONAL ELEMENTS TO INCLUDE

- One character doesn't descend the stairs.
- One of them dies very slowly.
- They are being recorded by surveillance cameras.

Horror Twist

What if one of the characters in the group knows exactly what's at the bottom of the stairs, and he's lured the rest of them down there to feed a creature that's desperate for human flesh? Make your readers trust this character so this twist comes as a surprise and they experience the same gut punch felt by your characters.

“What Are You Doing?”

SCENARIO

Your protagonist is visiting a family member. In the middle of the night, he hears a strange sound. He calls out, but no one responds. Then he hears the sound again. Instead of waking his loved one, he investigates. At first, nothing seems amiss. Maybe he misheard. He's about to head back to bed when he hears the sound again. It leads him to a door he's never seen, hidden behind a piece of furniture or under a heavy rug, or maybe he must crawl *through* the fridge.

BRAINSTORM

How close is your protagonist to his family? What do blood ties mean to him? If he found out he was related to someone capable of evil, how would he react? Does evil usually run in the family? Is homicidal psychosis a genetic trait?

WRITE

Write a scene where your protagonist wanders into a part of the house he never knew about, and when he finally reaches the end point, he sees the family member he's staying with. They are in the middle of a heinous act of your choice—anything from witchcraft to torture to murder. Maybe the family member is opening a portal to hell. Whatever your protagonist sees, it will haunt him forever.

Remember: Just because your protagonist sees his loved one doesn't mean the loved one sees your protagonist. Is it possible for him to retreat to the main part of the house without being detected? How much danger is he in right now?

OPTIONAL ELEMENTS TO INCLUDE

- Unsteady floorboards.
- Intense eye contact.
- Your protagonist suddenly gets sick.

Horror Twist

What if your protagonist tries to turn back but can't? Perhaps he has inadvertently walked into a cage (complete with rats, feces, and human remains), and he's trapped down there. When his family member finds him, he will be forced to deal with the consequences of his snooping.

Callbacks

What if something similar happened to your protagonist in the past? He saw a family member (one of his parents, an aunt or an uncle) doing something horrifying when he was younger, but he blocked it out. After what he witnesses in this scene, those memories come flooding back.

Wait Here

SCENARIO

Several children play hide-and-seek inside one of their homes. One of the kids finds a hidden door that opens into a part of the house they never knew existed. She tells her friends she's going to see what's in there. And she never returns.

BRAINSTORM

What are the general dynamics of this friend group? Who are the bravest and the most timid? Who is the leader, and who makes bad decisions? Make a list of the worst dangers they might face on the other side of that door and how they would each react.

WRITE

Write a scene where the missing child's friends debate what they should do next. Do they go through the door and look for their friend? Or do they get help and risk getting in trouble for doing something they shouldn't have?

OPTIONAL ELEMENTS TO INCLUDE

- An unexpected temptation.
- A severed limb.
- Someone gets bitten.

Horror Twist

What if the kid that lives here is lying when he says he's never seen this door before? What if he wants his friends to encounter a danger that lies within? How long can you delay revealing that he's a total psychopath?

Quick Writes

Set a timer for 15 minutes and do not stop writing until the timer goes off. Do not edit, cross out, or censor yourself. Write down every thought that comes to you.

1. Write a scene where your protagonist discovers a rabid animal in his home. He tries to find where the animal came from, but all the windows and doors are closed. It came from below. What else could be down there?
2. Write a scene where your protagonist meets with her former real estate agent, who asks if she's discovered the hidden room in her home yet, then adds: "I wouldn't go down there if I were you."
3. Your protagonist gets taken (by a monster, psycho, or paranormal creature) during the night. She wakes up in an underground lair. She hears the faint sounds of her family above, but they can't hear her. How does she escape?
4. There's a strange bump under the carpet in your protagonist's living room. He's never noticed it before. When he pulls up the rug to see what it is, he discovers a hidden door. Does he investigate alone?
5. Your protagonist is possessed suddenly by a ghost or demon. Write a scene where he creates a cavernous hole in the floor of his living room, kitchen, or bedroom. Whatever's down there is terrible: It could be a torture chamber, a tomb, or even hell itself.

IN THE MIDDLE OF NOWHERE

Have you ever been driving through a desolate area and wondered what would happen if your car broke down? How would you get help? Would you handle the situation calmly, or would your heart start racing? How long would it take you to reach a state of panic?

There's a reason so many horror stories take place In the Middle of Nowhere. It's not just because remote locations are scary (though that certainly heightens the creepy factor). The secret to the success of this trope is: no cell phones. The stakes of your story immediately ratchet up when you put your protagonist in a location where his cell phone is out of commission. If something bad happens, he can't reach out to a friend. If he encounters a monster, he can't notify the authorities. He can't even look up his own location to see how the hell to get to safety. He is completely and utterly on his own. And anything could be out here.

So, when something terrifying comes after him, he knows that help isn't on the way, and he's forced to face his trauma head-on. If he survives, he'll be grateful for everything he used to take for granted. His friends, his family, his personal health and safety. But mostly his phone.

Did You Hear That?

SCENARIO

Your characters are moving into a remote house. (Maybe they inherited it, or bought it sight unseen because they needed a retreat from the city. Or maybe they heard it was empty, so they're moving in uninvited.) The closest neighbor is miles away. A trip to the grocery store takes careful planning because it's an hour's drive. Which means it wasn't smart to ignore warnings of an oncoming storm. Now they're stuck without enough supplies to make it through the horrible weather. How will they get through this?

BRAINSTORM

What are the sounds of isolation? Brainstorm at least five unusual noises they might encounter inside the house and five strange noises they might hear outside. Think about what each noise might signify. How do you determine which sounds to worry about?

WRITE

Write a scene where your characters try to distract themselves from the storm outside. They do something quotidian like playing cards, working on a puzzle, or maybe even playing a game of truth or dare. But the whole tenor of the evening changes when they hear a sound outside and realize: *That isn't the storm.* Someone (or something) is outside, trying to get in.

Remember: Even if they want to leave, the weather outside is too treacherous. They're stuck here until things calm down. That is, unless the dangers move inside the house.

OPTIONAL ELEMENTS TO INCLUDE

- Something crashes through one of the windows.
- Maggots.
- Moldy food.

Horror Twist

What if your main protagonist goes out in the cold for too long and experiences hypothermia? Is it possible the other "person" trying to get in is a figment of his weather-addled brain? Could his sanity be breaking down just like the house? Is he the one who poses the real danger?

Callbacks

If this is all in your protagonist's imagination, find the moment when the transition from reality to fantasy occurs and his narration becomes unreliable. When your readers learn what's really going on, they'll want to go back and reread to find clues that point to his weakening mind.

I Swear, There Was Someone in This Room

SCENARIO

Your characters live on a remote island. One night, they crack open an old book belonging to the former occupant of the house. They notice photographs in the book and handwritten words in the margins. As they read the words out loud, they realize they're voicing a strange incantation of some kind. Why are the walls suddenly shaking?

BRAINSTORM

Who was the previous owner of this home, and what kind of evil witchcraft were they involved in? Come up with at least five ways this person harmed this island and how the island itself might respond if this person were ever resurrected.

WRITE

Write a scene where your protagonist sees a familiar stranger in her bedroom. The stranger disappears before your protagonist can alert anyone else, but she realizes they looked like the person from the book's photos. Could they be the home's previous occupant?

OPTIONAL ELEMENTS TO INCLUDE

- Heavy breathing.
- A note written in blood.
- An unusual stain on her sheets.

Horror Twist

This island is so remote that they don't have reliable Wi-Fi or phone service. If your protagonist sent for help from someone on the mainland, it could take weeks for her message to get to them. Will it be too late?

We Have to Get Out of Here Now!

SCENARIO

It's a postapocalyptic world where much of humanity is gone. Small pockets of survivors move in groups, looking for safety, resources, and other survivors. Your protagonist has fallen in with one of these groups and they've taken shelter in an abandoned mall, schoolhouse, or stadium. It's hard to trust people these days; most people only watch out for themselves.

BRAINSTORM

How many of your protagonist's loved ones are dead now? How many family members, lovers, and friends? Is there anyone in this group who reminds him of someone he lost? Quickly brainstorm one thing he likes about each of the members of his cobbled-together group. If he wants to survive this new world, he's going to need allies. Could he partner up with anyone here?

WRITE

Write a scene where your protagonist wakes up in the middle of the night to the sounds of a zombie (or other postapocalyptic creature) eating one of the members of his group. What does your protagonist do? How does he wake the others? Do they fight or flee?

Remember: Every zombie story follows its own set of rules. Yours can differ from others—but you need to stay consistent within your novel's universe. Think about the rules of the creatures in your story. How are they made? What are their strengths and weaknesses? What do they eat? Why do they kill? How difficult is it to kill them? Do they sleep? How fast are they?

OPTIONAL ELEMENTS TO INCLUDE

- A barricade.
- Blood dripping from a ceiling.
- A handmade weapon.

Horror Twist

Zombies aren't the only "undead" creatures in the world of your story. What if the apocalypse was triggered by a series of nuclear explosions that altered many of the life forms nearby? Some animals, and even some humans, are different now. It all depends on how close they were to the nuclear fallout. Some have been altered in horrific ways.

Callbacks

Maybe your protagonist is familiar with their shelter from the before times. What if he knows a secret route that he can use to help the others get to safety?

Quick Writes

Set a timer for 15 minutes and do not stop writing until the timer goes off. Do not edit, cross out, or censor yourself. Write down every thought that comes to you.

1. Your protagonist's car breaks down on a remote highway. Write a scene where a seemingly kind stranger pulls over to help. Your protagonist wants to trust him, but there's something slightly off about this guy.
2. A group of friends get lost on a hike in the woods. Write a scene where they stumble upon a secret ceremony. It could be a coven of witches, a group of Satanists, or a cult initiation. The friends don't want to get involved, but then someone hears them.
3. Your protagonist wakes up, groggy and disoriented, tied up in the trunk of a car. A masked stranger dumps him out and drives off. Write a scene where he tries to figure out where he is—and if he has any company out here.
4. Your protagonist signs up for a mysterious, televised contest to get out of debt. She is delivered to a remote island. Write a scene where the show's host explains that if she can survive the island's supernatural inhabitants for the duration of the show, her debt will disappear.
5. Your newlywed protagonists go to a luxurious resort for their honeymoon. Write a scene where they discover that everyone else at the resort is dead.

GUESS WHO'S FOR DINNER

It's always nice to have a homemade meal with friends. Who doesn't like a glass of wine, some scintillating conversation, and a delicious meal cooked to perfection? Unless *you're* on the menu. That might sour the evening and make you wish you hadn't accepted the night's invitation.

The scariest thing about cannibals is they aren't merely an invention of fiction. When you read about vampires, demonic possession, or other scary paranormal stories, you can always calm your nerves by reminding yourself: *This isn't real.* But cannibals? They live among us. They run errands, pay taxes, and play pickleball. Your neighbor could be a cannibal. Or maybe the bartender at your favorite dive bar, or even someone you implicitly trust, like your family doctor. There's no way to tell who's a cannibal until he's preparing to serve you to his dinner guests.

Maybe that's what makes cannibalism such a delectable horror trope that's bound to get a visceral reaction out of your readers. It's horrifying to think that someone might take pleasure in the act of eating another human, and yet: What if?

It's also a twist writers frequently turn to because it's ripe with metaphor. You can talk about capitalism, overconsumption, status climbing in the workplace, the gender divide, and the power dynamics of any relationship. Who is the eater and who is the eaten? Only one can survive.

Needs More Spice

SCENARIO

Your protagonist is among a group being held captive by an antagonist of your choice—anything from a serial killer to a deranged family member to a ghost who's taken corporeal form because she's pissed that people are living in her former home. Your protagonist is alarmed when he notices that one of the other captives has mysteriously gone missing.

BRAINSTORM

How many people are being held captive? Think about all the ways they might bond as a result of the trauma. How quickly does your protagonist connect with the other captives, and how do they help each other stay hopeful that they might get out of here?

WRITE

Write a scene where the antagonist feeds a nice meal to the captives, and at some point (before they start eating, midway through the meal, or—if you want things to get especially twisted—after they're done), your protagonist learns that they're eating the missing captive.

Remember: They might not have known each other before they found themselves in this terrible situation, but your protagonist bonded with the missing captive quickly. The loss of a friend would hit him hard in any scenario, but *eating* his friend makes the whole situation far worse than he thought things could get. This might drive him to madness.

OPTIONAL ELEMENTS TO INCLUDE

- Alcohol.
- Fancy table settings.
- A detached fingernail.

Horror Twist

How does your protagonist find out what he's really eating? What if he recognizes something in the food that is undeniably his friend? Perhaps he sees the faint lines of a tattoo in an appetizer. Or he bites down on something hard, spits it out, and sees that it's unmistakably a golden tooth. How twisted can you get?

Callbacks

Think about what the antagonist wants from your protagonist. Did the dead captive refuse to play the antagonist's game? What can your protagonist learn from this, and how can he change his behavior to ensure that he doesn't become next week's midnight special?

Tell Me You're Lying

SCENARIO

Your protagonist helps former addicts get their lives together. She tries to maintain professional boundaries, but she's quietly obsessed with one man who is both creepy and compelling.

BRAINSTORM

Your protagonist thinks about this former addict more than she probably should. How does she describe him to her friends? What does she share, and what does she keep private? Why does she need to keep some of her feelings secret?

WRITE

Write a scene where your protagonist learns that the man wasn't addicted to drugs or alcohol. His problem wasn't quite so common. He was addicted to the taste of human flesh.

Remember: People have a great capacity for ignoring their instincts, especially when learning something bad about someone they like. Does any justification take place?

OPTIONAL ELEMENTS TO INCLUDE

- They talk so long that it's dark when they finally walk to their cars.
- Your protagonist thinks he's joking.
- She gives him a ride home.

Horror Twist

Think about the bad choices a person makes when they have intense feelings for someone. How many mistakes does your protagonist make before she's in too deep? What if she agrees to try human flesh, just to see what the fuss is about, and it makes her very, very ill?

"I Don't Eat Someone Unless I Really Like Them"

SCENARIO

Your protagonist has dinner plans at a Michelin-starred restaurant. She's been looking forward to eating here for a long time. It could be a date, or a visit with a family member she hasn't seen in years, or a reunion with an old friend. She notices her fellow diner is acting strangely as he asks for an off-menu chef's special. She senses he's hiding something from her.

BRAINSTORM

Write the moments leading up to this dinner. What did your protagonist do to prepare? Did she talk to anyone else about her expectations? What does she think of this person? Will she be disappointed if the night doesn't go as planned? What stresses and anxieties in her life might make her especially hopeful for a pleasant evening? Clarify what's personally at stake.

WRITE

Write this dinner scene. Let everything go exceptionally well at first. Your protagonist is happy to be here. This is what she needed. Her defenses are down, and her companion is feeling comfortable too—maybe too comfortable. He tells her the truth when she asks him about the secret chef's special, and she's horrified to learn her dinner once had a name (like Dave, or Javier, or Samantha). She's about to completely lose it.

Remember: Your protagonist really likes the person she's dining with, so she might not believe him at first. But who would joke about something like culinary cannibalism? Even if he backtracks and denies it, she feels revolted and scared. Unfortunately, she's outnumbered here. If she plays this wrong, she will end up on the menu next.

OPTIONAL ELEMENTS TO INCLUDE

- Wine. A lot of it.
- A locked door.
- A story about a scar.

Horror Twist

It's unlikely your protagonist will get out of here alive. As soon as she agreed to attend this dinner, she signed her own death certificate. As that reality begins to dawn on her and her survival instincts kick in, think about all the tactics she might use to try to escape.

Callbacks

Your protagonist's dinner companion wants to eat her. If she thinks through their past together, can she connect with him in a way that might make him lose his appetite?

Quick Writes

Set a timer for 15 minutes and do not stop writing until the timer goes off. Do not edit, cross out, or censor yourself. Write down every thought that comes to you.

1. Your antagonist is hungry. Write a scene where he follows a stranger through a busy area, discreetly hunting them before going in for the kill.
2. Write a scene where your protagonist cooks for friends. She needs to get all the components right, timing things so the sides are ready with the main course. Does an adult male take longer to cook than chicken?
3. Write a scene where your protagonist goes on a date and passes out. When he wakes up, he's in a walk-in freezer with several half-eaten human carcasses. How will he get out of here alive?
4. Write a scene where your protagonist drops in on her adult son because she's worried about him. When she starts snooping, he hopes she won't look in the fridge.
5. Write a scene where one of your characters attends a group therapy session and admits he's curious about the taste of human flesh. Based on the poor reactions from the group, he knows he has to kill them before they turn him in.

YOU'RE BEING WATCHED

Imagine this: You're staying in a hotel room when you notice a small, almost imperceptible, red light behind the mirror. You move in closer to investigate. You stare at the tiny dot and suddenly realize: Someone is recording you.

Or: There's a knock on your door. But when you open it, no one's there. All you find is an envelope on the welcome mat. Inside the envelope, there's a note that describes your most private thoughts. Things you've never shared with anyone else. Who wrote this, and how did they get in your head?

Or what if: You receive an email marked Urgent. Attached, you find several photos of yourself—photos of moments when you thought you were alone. But someone else was there. Spying on you. The invasion of privacy makes you feel sick. You're Being Watched by someone who wants to harm you.

There are endless ways these stories could go. When your protagonist discovers she's being watched, she might not believe it at first. But it will unnerve her. She'll try to figure out who it is and what they want. She might even go after them to try to stop them. She's playing a dangerous game, and she's at an immediate disadvantage. How does she regain control when she doesn't even know who's taken it away from her?

I Saw a Light in the Dark 

SCENARIO

Your protagonist is at a fancy resort. Beautiful views, luxurious rooms, incredible food, attentive staff, friendly guests. But there's something amiss that she can't put her finger on. Everything about this place is perfect. Almost *too* perfect. Your protagonist doesn't want to bring up her concerns, but she's worried something sinister is going on behind the scenes.

BRAINSTORM

Your protagonist is right to be afraid. This resort holds many secrets. Come up with a backstory for the resort. Who owns it, who works here, and what do they want from their unsuspecting guests? Are they performing secret experiments on the people who stay here? Are they looking for specific individuals who meet certain criteria needed for a spell or ritual? Are they stealing souls? Come up with the what, why, and how of their diabolic plans.

WRITE

Your protagonist sees a blinking light in the middle of the night. Write a scene where she tells her partner there are hidden cameras in their room. When they investigate, they don't find anything suspicious. But she knows what she saw. Now she's even more upset than she was before.

Remember: If they're being recorded, it might not be safe to openly look for cameras. Is there anything your protagonist can do to make her search less obvious?

OPTIONAL ELEMENTS TO INCLUDE

- Your protagonist's phone is missing.
- She feels woozy.
- She catches her partner in a lie.

Horror Twist

What if your protagonist's partner brought her here on purpose? What if he's being paid a finder's fee to deliver her here? Think about how long they've been together and how much of a betrayal it would be if he turned out to be a bad guy.

Callbacks

When they first arrive at the resort, your protagonist and her partner are given a tour. Include a moment when the concierge says something that makes your protagonist pause. Later, when she finds out what's going on here, she'll wish she had listened to her gut instincts about this place.

What's That Buzzing Sound? 

SCENARIO

Nnnn. There's this awful buzzing sound. *Nnnn.* Your protagonist hears it everywhere he goes. *Nnnnn.* Is it coming from his neighbor's house? *NnnnNNn.* Are they doing construction outside? *NnnNNNnn.* Is there something wrong with his car? *Nnnn.* Somehow the noise isn't coming from anywhere—but, at the same time, it's everywhere.

BRAINSTORM

What would you do if you kept hearing noises that no one else was able to hear? Do some research into the psychological effects of noise pollution.

WRITE

Your protagonist decides the sounds are coming from inside his head. What if someone implanted a recording device in his skull so they could keep tabs on him and watch his every move? Write a scene where he tries to dig the foreign object out of his flesh.

OPTIONAL ELEMENTS TO INCLUDE

- A screwdriver.
- He feels a foreign object under his skin.
- The voice of the Divine.

Horror Twist

Think about the sound your protagonist hears. Is it always the same, or are there variations? What if he begins to identify various tones and recognize patterns? Could the sounds be trying to tell him something? What if they want him to do something for them—something evil?

“I’m Looking Through You”

SCENARIO

Everywhere your protagonist goes, someone watches. At the grocery store, she sees someone staring from the other checkout line. When she goes to work, two strangers wait for her in the parking lot—but they don’t approach her, they just watch. When she meets friends for a drink, someone stares through the window. They never attempt to harm her, but their constant presence is freaking her out.

BRAINSTORM

Why is she so unsettled by merely being *looked* at? Think about the psychological damage someone could inflict on you just by watching you. There’s a suggestion of malice, a vague threat, even the possibility of violence. It’s so easy to fill in the blanks and become obsessed with the idea that you’re in danger.

WRITE

Write a scene where your protagonist confronts one of her stalkers, but they deny everything. They say they weren’t looking at her, claim not to have any awareness of her, and act as if your protagonist is the one bothering them. No matter what she says, they hold firm. Take your protagonist from being unnerved to a state of paranoid rage.

Remember: This has been going on for a long time. Your protagonist’s emotions are close to the surface. She’s been holding so much in. It won’t take long for her to unravel.

OPTIONAL ELEMENTS TO INCLUDE

- A hostile shove.
- Someone calls the police.
- A choked sob.

Horror Twist

Are the watchers part of a supernatural cult? Are they aliens? Are they figments of your protagonist's imagination? Do they have powers? Or what if they're just regular people who've chosen her at random and have decided to ruin her life just because they can?

Callbacks

How many times does your protagonist notice she's being watched before she finally gets up the courage to fight back? Has she tried before today but stopped herself because she lost her nerve?

Quick Writes

Set a timer for 15 minutes and do not stop writing until the timer goes off. Do not edit, cross out, or censor yourself. Write down every thought that comes to you.

1. Your protagonist is renting out the accessory dwelling unit in her backyard to a new tenant. She wakes up and sees him outside her window, looking in. Write a scene where she confronts him and is frightened by his reaction.
2. Your protagonist notices a new surveillance camera in his office. When he goes to lunch, he notices another new camera. When he's walking home after work, he notices several more. Write a scene where he has a public meltdown.
3. Your protagonist notices two huge eyes staring at him from a new billboard facing his office window. Write a scene where he confesses to a friend that he believes the billboard is alive and is keeping track of everything he does.
4. A stranger accuses your protagonist of following her. Your protagonist is innocent, but now he's weirdly curious about this woman. Write a scene where he secretly follows her, even though he senses this won't end well.
5. Your protagonist is afraid she's slowly transforming into a creature of some sort. She has powerful feral instincts. Write a scene where she is approached by a stranger who says, "We've been watching you. You're one of us."

CURSE

Your protagonist may not be evil, but he's far from admirable. He used to be a good guy, but he's been worn down by the challenges in his life. He's overwhelmed by responsibilities at work. His family doesn't appreciate him enough. When he isn't yelling at them, he's neglecting them. He used to dream, but now he just thinks about all the obligations that weigh him down. He always has his head buried in his phone. He isn't nice to strangers anymore. He doesn't even tip the barista. All these little, unkind actions add up. They harden his heart. But one day his rudeness catches up to him.

Maybe he cuts off a stranger—who turns out to be an ancient witch with incredible powers. Or he lashes out at a loved one in a restaurant and makes a scene in front of a group of strangers—including a disgruntled god who's disgusted by his casual cruelty. They look at him and think, *This is a man who needs to learn a lesson.* That's when the Curse happens.

Here's the thing about witches, gods, and similar malevolent creatures: They do not forgive and forget. If your protagonist gets on their bad side, they will cause him misfortune with glee. He's about to discover that being cursed is far worse than any of the petty troubles he's dealing with now. This is going to be a difficult (and potentially deadly) lesson.

There's No Escaping Your Destiny

SCENARIO

If you're a good enough person, the universe will reward you, right? That's what your protagonist always thought, but bad things keep happening to her. She's recently dealt with some (or all) of these nightmares: Her home is flooded; she totals her car; she chips her front tooth; her dog dies; she loses her job; a drunk driver crashes into her living room; she's developing a massive tumor in her neck; and so on. Why can't she get a break?

BRAINSTORM

Your protagonist used to believe in karma. Not so much anymore. If she were to seek professional help, what advice might she receive from a therapist, shaman, psychic, priest, or even an exorcist? Think through the extreme actions she might take to counteract her run of bad luck.

WRITE

Write a scene where your protagonist goes to a family gathering and one of her elders pulls her aside to talk about her troubles. At first, your protagonist thinks they want to lend a sympathetic ear. But it turns out this family member has a message for her: "You've inherited the family curse." They aren't speaking metaphorically.

Remember: If it's a family curse, your protagonist knows many others who have dealt with this nightmare. She may go to them for help, but they treat her like she has the plague. A curse taints you like that. Whatever your protagonist must do to reverse the curse, make it ugly and painful.

OPTIONAL ELEMENTS TO INCLUDE

- A leech.
- An elder dies painfully and suddenly.
- Choking.

Horror Twist

Your protagonist's body is revolting against her. She feels like she's falling apart. What if she literally is? If she doesn't find a cure for this curse soon, there won't be anything left of her.

Callbacks

Think about where the curse originated. What family member can she blame for her current condition? If they're still alive, will she fancy a little taste of revenge?

Her Blood's on Your Hands

SCENARIO

Your life can change in an instant. Unfortunately, you can change other people's lives in an instant too, especially if you're distracted and accidentally commit manslaughter.

BRAINSTORM

Your protagonist has had an awful day. Make a list of everything that's gone wrong. She's about to do something that makes everything worse. What's her headspace like in the moment before?

WRITE

Your protagonist accidentally kills someone. Maybe she's texting and driving when she slams into a pedestrian. Maybe, running late for a meeting, she clumsily pushes over an elderly woman who hits her head on the pavement and dies. Maybe she serves her nephew a salad with nuts in it, forgetting his deadly allergy. Whatever she's done has filled her with guilt. Write a scene where a loved one of the deceased inflicts a terrible curse upon her.

OPTIONAL ELEMENTS TO INCLUDE

- A blood stain that won't go away.
- Clawing at someone's eyes.
- Your protagonist loses a tooth or fingernail.

Horror Twist

The curse can be anything. What loss would hurt your protagonist most? What's the most terrifying way she could experience that loss? Think about how you can keep turning the screw. As your story goes on, let the curse's effects multiply.

The Only Way Out Is Death 

SCENARIO

Your protagonist is a morally corrupt dirtbag. He's hurt so many people that he doesn't even know who cursed him. How would he begin to narrow down the suspects? But he knows one thing: He isn't going to let his life be derailed by a curse, no matter how bad it is.

BRAINSTORM

Write a brief biography of your protagonist, outlining the many sins he has committed. How many people hate him? Who would be motivated to destroy him? Is there anyone he doesn't suspect of cursing him, and if so, why?

WRITE

Your protagonist's life is falling apart because of a curse. He suspects the only way to reverse the curse is through death—not *his* death, but the death of the person who inflicted this pain on him. Write a scene where he seeks out one of his enemies and brutally murders them. Afterwards, nothing changes—which means he didn't get the right guy. He's going to have to kill again.

Remember: Your protagonist is a bad guy. But has he murdered before, or is this the first time? What's his style? Careless and messy or brutally efficient? Think about how his desperation affects his actions. He's both the victim of horror and the perpetrator of it.

OPTIONAL ELEMENTS TO INCLUDE

- A moment of resurrection.
- A bludgeoning.
- A witness who must be killed too.

Horror Twist

Think about the intentions of the person who cursed your protagonist. What do they want him to learn? What do they want him to regret about the way he's lived his life? And what if they've included a failsafe in the curse, designed to make sure he ultimately feels that regret? From now on, every time he hurts someone (either emotionally or physically), the curse will deepen.

Quick Writes

Set a timer for 15 minutes and do not stop writing until the timer goes off. Do not edit, cross out, or censor yourself. Write down every thought that comes to you.

1. Your protagonist is cursed with the gift of immortality. Write a scene where he survives a massive car crash and it dawns on him that immortality isn't pain-free.
2. Your protagonist suffers from a terrible curse: She can predict the death of every person she spends time with. She's avoided her loved ones ever since this curse began. She knows she couldn't stand the pain of having their fates revealed. Write a scene where she encounters one of her parents and is horrified by the grim death she envisions.
3. Your protagonist is cursed to become the thing he hates most. Write a scene where he wakes up to discover that the changes have begun. They aren't pretty.
4. Your protagonist is cursed to a life of eternal loneliness. Write a scene where he makes a desperate attempt to connect with someone but they are savagely cruel to him.
5. Your gluttonous protagonist is cursed to never experience pleasure again. Write a scene where she overdoses on something she used to love (perhaps food, sex, or a combination of the two).

THEY'RE HERE

Death is at your door. He might look like a deliveryman, a charity worker, or a friendly new neighbor. But the smile's an act. He wants to torture and kill you.

He doesn't have to knock. He might shimmy a lock, slip in through an open window, or break down the front door with blunt force. He isn't deterred by your alarm system or the "Warning: Attack Dog" sign. If he wants to come in, nothing will stop him.

But sometimes he does knock, which is more unnerving because he's maintaining the illusion of politeness. He might feign weakness, asking if he can sit for a minute because he's been in the sun all day. He wants you to call his bluff and turn him away. Then you're the one escalating the situation. Suddenly you need a lesson in manners. He was planning to teach you this lesson either way, but now you've given him a reason to act. It's time for you to understand that he belongs here. He's in charge now.

Home invasion stories are terrifying, because they can happen anywhere. Your readers will envision your story happening in their own neighborhood. It could happen to their loved ones. It could happen to themselves. They're going to wonder if they'd handle it as well as your protagonist does. Would they fight or flee? Would they be able to take their home back? Would *you*?

"You Can't Hide from Us Anymore"

SCENARIO

Your wealthy protagonists have spent months planning a dream vacation, but they had to cancel their trip at the last minute due to a work conflict or family emergency. The intruders didn't get that memo, though; they thought the house would be empty. Their plan was to get in, take the valuables, and get out—no one was supposed to get hurt. Unfortunately, the plan is about to go awry.

BRAINSTORM

How prepared are your protagonists for a home invasion, both mentally and physically? Is this something they're afraid of? Is it something they talk about and plan for? Do they own a gun or any other weapons? Do they have a panic room? What is their security system like, and how hard would it be for the intruders to disable it? Visualize each room in the house and brainstorm what everyday objects could potentially be used as weapons in an emergency.

WRITE

Two characters (anyone from spouses to siblings to parent and child) are hiding from home invaders when they discover their hiding spot is compromised. The invaders will find them soon. But if they come out of hiding, they put themselves in harm's way. Write a scene where they plan to go on the offensive and attack the intruders before the intruders can attack them.

Remember: Your protagonists are outnumbered. Maybe one is afraid to leave the hiding place, even though she understands they can't stay here safely much longer. The stakes in this moment are life or death. What does the other character say to convince her to move?

OPTIONAL ELEMENTS TO INCLUDE

- An alarm.
- A broken limb.
- An incantation.

Horror Twist

The intruders think they're breaking into a normal home inhabited by average humans, but what if they don't have the whole story? What if the residents of this home are secretly vampires, werewolves, witches, demons, or other powerful supernatural beings? Think about how you might reveal the true nature of your protagonists in the most shocking manner. The intruders have no idea how bad things are about to get.

Smile—You're Dead

SCENARIO

Your protagonist is running errands—anything from grocery shopping to dropping off a package at the post office. He notices a stranger taking a photo of him. The stranger says something threatening. It's so jarring that he isn't sure he heard correctly, but the stranger is gone before he can clarify or find out who this person is. The whole encounter is uncomfortable and upsetting. It leaves your protagonist unsettled for the rest of the day.

BRAINSTORM

Think about how one photograph can change a person's life. What might your protagonist be caught doing that could be misinterpreted, manipulated, and made to look much worse than it was in the moment? Is it possible to destroy a person with one photo?

WRITE

Write a scene where your protagonist sees something on his dining room table that wasn't there before. It's an envelope containing photos the stranger took of him. How did it get here, and what does the stranger want from him? The stranger's threat suddenly takes on even more meaning. Was the stranger inside your protagonist's home? Is he still here?

Remember: Your protagonist might have something he's trying to hide. How far would he go to keep his skeletons in the closet? What does your protagonist look like when he's on the edge?

OPTIONAL ELEMENTS TO INCLUDE

- A panic attack.
- A photo taken inside your protagonist's home.
- A recorded message.

Horror Twist

What if one of the photos shows your protagonist committing murder? He laughs it off, at first. It's obviously an altered photo, since he's never killed anyone. He doesn't even recognize the person he's supposedly killing. But then he meets someone new and recognizes them from the photo. Is it possible the photo's showing him something he's going to do in the future?

"They Took Me in the Middle of the Night"

SCENARIO

Your protagonist is at a bed-and-breakfast with a loved one. He wakes up one morning and feels different. He notices strange markings on his skin. He also has an unusual sensation in his body, like there's something foreign under his skin. Whatever it is, it's alive.

BRAINSTORM

What might the markings mean? If someone put them there, think about what they were intended to signify. Is it possible your protagonist was branded? Why?

WRITE

Your protagonist thinks he was abducted in the middle of the night. He thinks the owners of the B&B aren't who they say they are. When he shares his theory with his loved one(s), they're skeptical. But he's certain something's *off* about all this.

Remember: Your protagonist is normally a level-headed guy. But nothing like this has ever happened before, and he's beginning to doubt everything he feels or encounters.

OPTIONAL ELEMENTS TO INCLUDE

- A growing sense of doom.
- A voice in the darkness.
- Your protagonist has a seizure.

Horror Twist

Before your protagonist checked into this B&B, someone told him not to stay here. He shrugged the guy off as "crazy" and ignored his warnings. But now others are looking at your protagonist like something is wrong with *him*.

Quick Writes

Set a timer for 15 minutes and do not stop writing until the timer goes off. Do not edit, cross out, or censor yourself. Write down every thought that comes to you.

1. Write a scene where a family barricades themselves in one room as the rest of their home is overtaken by zombies, demons, or aliens. What your characters don't know is the room isn't as secure as they think.
2. Your protagonist is the last one in the office late Friday night. Write a scene where she lets a stranger in—maybe a delivery man or a police officer. This stranger has no intention of ever leaving.
3. Your protagonist chats with someone on a dating app. The conversation turns weird and scary. Write a scene where he goes to block his romantic "match" and sees a GPS notification: *Your match is zero feet away*. He feels a hand on his shoulder.
4. An evil entity has invaded the school where your protagonist works, but he won't let this diabolical force get its hands on any of the students. Write a scene where your protagonist constructs a weapon using everyday classroom items and fights back.
5. Write a scene where a violent gang breaks into your protagonist's home. She hides in a tight space, desperately hoping they'll leave before they find her.

MYSTERIOUS DEATH

There's only one experience every living soul has in common: We're all going to die. You might argue that death is the great unifier. But not all deaths are created equal. In the case of a Mysterious Death, the sadness is weighed down by a heavy blanket of questions. The search for answers can drive your characters to despair. And it just might send them down dark and unexpected paths that are hard to come back from.

How do you deal with losing someone too young, before it's their time? What about when there's something inexplicably *off* about the circumstances of their death? You can't quite put your finger on it, but you just know something isn't right. Or what if your loved one's body is missing and you've been robbed of the closure you so desperately need? How do you move on?

Some characters don't. Some characters never stop seeking answers. Some even embrace their misery. It's times like these when the distance between our world and the next can suddenly contract. When the veil lifts, who knows what might happen? Suddenly the idea that we're all going to die starts to resonate even more deeply for your protagonist: If they aren't careful, they'll experience a Mysterious Death of their own.

She Can't Be Gone; I Just Talked to Her

SCENARIO

Your protagonist gets an unexpected visit from a loved one. This isn't a good time, so they have a hurried conversation. Maybe your protagonist is rude, or she cuts the visit short. She takes for granted that they'll be able to continue talking tomorrow. That's a decision she'll regret.

BRAINSTORM

Think about what the loved one wants to tell your protagonist but doesn't get a chance to say. Write a version of the scene that goes perfectly. Then strip away some key details. Make your readers feel the incompleteness in their conversation. Unfinished business.

WRITE

Write a scene where your protagonist receives the news that her loved one actually died—yesterday. Before their visit. Now your protagonist is determined to talk to her again. She will do anything to get that moment back—that visit from the other side. She will even put herself in harm's way, if necessary.

OPTIONAL ELEMENTS TO INCLUDE

- A chill in the air.
- A lie.
- A difficult request.

Horror Twist

What if the loved one has been changed by death? What if they've been influenced by demonic forces from the underworld? Think about why they're here and what they want from your protagonist.

I Can Still Feel Him with Me 

SCENARIO

Your protagonist is still mourning the death of a dear loved one (a spouse, a sibling, a parent, a best friend, or perhaps a child) who died of mysterious causes. On the anniversary of his death, she visits his grave. For a moment, she can sense him with her. But instead of being comforted by that thought, she gets an overwhelming feeling that something is wrong.

BRAINSTORM

Think about her connection to this loved one. Make a quick list of things they had in common: their favorite memories together, inside jokes they shared, and any other symbols of their deep connection. What secrets did they share with each other and no one else? What did she love most about him? If your protagonist ever encountered him again (after his death), what are the signs that would tip her off and tell her, without a doubt, that her loved one had returned?

WRITE

Write a scene where your protagonist confides in a friend that she thinks her dead loved one is still here, and she's worried about him. You decide *how* she thinks he's returned. (Is he a spirit in the ether? Has he returned in some other form? What if she thinks he's somehow inside her, and maybe she even thinks he can control her actions?) Does the friend go along with it, even though they think it might be a grief-induced delusion? Or does the friend get professional help for your protagonist?

Remember: Your protagonist is still in mourning, and she wants nothing more than to be reunited with her loved one. How far would she go to make such a reunion possible? Think about how dangerous these emotions might be and how they might manifest.

OPTIONAL ELEMENTS TO INCLUDE

- A confession.
- A bloody wound.
- A spontaneous act of destruction.

Horror Twist

What if your protagonist accidentally opens a portal to the other side when she visits her dead loved one's grave? When her loved one returns, the portal stays open. Now spirits are coming through at an alarming rate, and most of them aren't the peaceful, happy, loving kind.

You're Next

SCENARIO

Your protagonist is mourning a loved one. He's gotten into the habit of visiting places his loved one used to frequent (her favorite restaurant, her old school, her neighborhood bar, etc.) because it makes him feel close to her. But then he starts to sense her presence. Is he going crazy, or could she still be here? He feels like she's trying to tell him something.

BRAINSTORM

What's the worst possible way to die? Think about the loved one's final moments. Put yourself in her head and write a stream-of-consciousness monologue of her last few minutes. What were her regrets at the end, and how much pain did she endure? Take this a step further and envision her first moments in the afterlife. How would she react if she suddenly found herself burning in hell?

WRITE

Write a scene where your protagonist encounters the spirit of his dead loved one. Maybe it's difficult for her to communicate with him, and it takes a while before he realizes what's happening. There might be a moment of joy when they finally connect. But then twist the scene with a terrible revelation: She's here to warn him about how he's going to die.

Remember: The loved one died under mysterious circumstances. Decide for yourself if those details are a mystery to her as well, or if she's able to shed light on what happened. If the loved one was murdered, is it possible the same killer is coming after your protagonist?

OPTIONAL ELEMENTS TO INCLUDE

- A glitch in time.
- Physical contact.
- A code that needs to be solved.

Horror Twist

What if the dead loved one can communicate only haltingly, because she's actively decomposing? Death has changed her in horrifying ways, and words don't come easily. Maybe it's incredibly painful for her to be here and awful for your protagonist to see her like this.

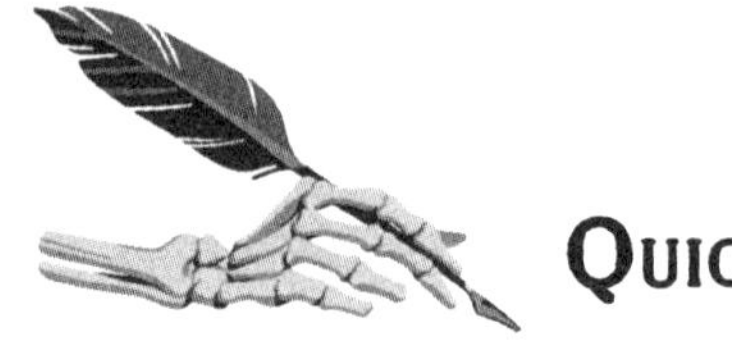

Quick Writes

Set a timer for 15 minutes and do not stop writing until the timer goes off. Do not edit, cross out, or censor yourself. Write down every thought that comes to you.

1. Your protagonist has discovered a fissure in space that serves as a portal to the afterlife. Write a scene where he gets sucked through the portal and finds himself confronted with his worst fears come to life.
2. Write a chase scene where your protagonist desperately tries to get away from a loved one who has returned from the dead in an altered state. (Perhaps he is aggressively violent and cruel; perhaps he inhabits other people's bodies.)
3. Write a scene where your protagonist meets with a medium to communicate with his dead spouse or child but something goes terribly wrong. The dead loved one wants to punish him for a painful betrayal.
4. Write a scene where your protagonist witnesses a murder, but when she reports it to the police, the body is gone. Did she *really* see what she thought she saw? And why does she keep seeing the body?
5. Your protagonist was violently murdered by a stranger. Write a scene where she comes back to haunt her killer and discovers that her anger is infectious. When she touches one of the living, they immediately grow violent.

DEMONIC DOLLS

Your protagonist hates that doll. Every time she goes into her daughter's room, she feels like it's staring at her. It seems to have a mind of its own, moving to different spots, causing mischief in the night. When your protagonist tells her loved ones a sinister doll may be in their midst, they shut her down. "It's just a doll," they say, but she feels like they're gaslighting her. She senses the doll wants to communicate something. It has a message, or maybe a warning, that it needs to deliver. Or what if it wants to compel your protagonist to do something bad? The only thing your protagonist knows for sure is that if she doesn't get rid of that doll soon, it might be too late.

Demonic dolls are a staple of horror because dolls are supposed to represent innocence, but their limp, lifeless bodies take on a creepy energy in the darkness of night. Depending on the needs of your story, any doll could go bad: a baby doll, a rag doll, a ventriloquist dummy, a puppet made of felt, a porcelain doll, a stuffed teddy bear, Russian nesting dolls, even action figures.

Every doll has a backstory, and they all come with baggage. Use that to your advantage when you write about Demonic Dolls. Tap into your readers' expectations about the comfort and joy that a doll is meant to provide, and then have gleeful, gory fun subverting those expectations.

Why Would I Hurt You?

SCENARIO

Every morning, your protagonist wakes up with bruises, cuts, scratches, and even little bite marks on her skin. She's afraid to admit this to anyone, but she suspects that one of her daughter's dolls is doing the damage. She can't explain it rationally; it's just a vibe the doll gives off.

BRAINSTORM

Come up with a backstory for this evil doll. How did it become sentient? What does it want? What does it need to survive? Does it have to follow any rules? Is it protecting your protagonist's daughter, or does it have more sinister intentions? What if it grows more powerful the more pain it inflicts?

WRITE

Write a scene where your protagonist talks to her child's doll. She's surprised when the doll talks back, but nothing the doll says is cute. It doesn't take long for your protagonist to realize her family is in danger.

OPTIONAL ELEMENTS TO INCLUDE

- An accusation.
- A threat.
- A secret revealed.

Horror Twist

What if your protagonist does some digging and discovers that this doll has had a long, violent past? It's left dozens of bodies in its wake. Perhaps this is just the beginning of another reign of terror . . .

Bury Her As Deep As You Can

SCENARIO

A doll has come to life, and it's wreaking havoc on an unsuspecting community. Decide what kind of doll it is (a stuffed animal, baby doll, action figure, teddy bear, puppet, mannequin, wooden boy, and so on), then think about how your protagonist is connected to this once-inanimate object. At this point in your story, the doll has done a lot of damage. Your protagonist has been hurt by this doll in more ways than one.

BRAINSTORM

What does the doll want? Do a deep dive into the doll's psychology. How did it come to life, what powers does it possess, what rules does it have to follow, and how can it be defeated? Does it hold a grudge against your protagonist for holding it captive for so long?

WRITE

Your protagonist hates this damned doll and will do anything in his power to destroy it. Write a series of scenes where your protagonist tries to get rid of the doll but everything he does fails. Is the doll indestructible? What's your protagonist missing? What does he need to do to finally break out of the doll's damaging orbit?

OPTIONAL ELEMENTS TO INCLUDE

- An incantation that doesn't work.
- The doll impersonates one of your protagonist's dead loved ones.
- A broken bone.

Horror Twist

The doll is possessed by a demon. What if this demon knows a shameful secret your protagonist has been trying to keep hidden? How might the demonic doll use this ill-gotten information to harm your protagonist?

Callbacks

What if the doll came with a set of instructions? Could the answer to the doll's destruction be hidden somewhere in the fine print?

"I Know You Lied to Me"

SCENARIO

In the wake of a terrible loss, your protagonist purchased a replica doll to replace a lost loved one. The doll could be a fill-in for a dead spouse, child, or parent. But instead of finding comfort in the doll, your protagonist is disturbed by how often it seems to go off script as it takes on its own personality. Something that was supposed to soothe has become alarmingly creepy.

BRAINSTORM

Get inside your protagonist's head and imagine why she thought this doll would be a good idea. What does she miss most about her dead loved one? In how many ways has her grief ricocheted throughout her life? What's the best possible outcome of inviting this doll into her home, and what's the worst outcome? Clarify for yourself why and how she got here.

WRITE

Write a scene where the doll accuses your protagonist of a deep betrayal. When your protagonist argues that the doll is mistaken, the doll doubles down. Is the doll gaslighting her? Maybe the doll is so persuasive that your protagonist even begins to doubt her own story and wonder if the doll might be right. Let the doll's mind games get her all twisted up inside.

Remember: This doll looks, acts (for the most part), and sounds exactly like your protagonist's dead loved one. This accusation should cut like a knife, and it might also bring up emotional wounds that your protagonist mistakenly thought she had already healed from.

OPTIONAL ELEMENTS TO INCLUDE

- A bite of flesh.
- A tender caress.
- Shattered glass.

Horror Twist

What if the doll isn't pretending to be your protagonist's loved one, but instead they really, truly *are* the loved one, come back to life through a perverse deal with the Devil? In death, the loved one has begun to embrace their worst impulses. They have no filter. It's like their shadow self has come out to play.

Callbacks

Your protagonist might try to remind the doll about happy times she shared with her loved one, but the doll finds a way to twist them into bad memories.

Quick Writes

Set a timer for 15 minutes and do not stop writing until the timer goes off. Do not edit, cross out, or censor yourself. Write down every thought that comes to you.

1. Write a scene where your protagonist tries to destroy a vengeful doll but discovers his nemesis is stronger than he thought. Instead of killing the doll, he ends up putting an innocent bystander in harm's way.
2. Write a scene where an army of demonic dolls attacks your protagonist's home and your protagonist does something drastic (and spectacular) to fight them off.
3. Write a scene where a possessed stuffed animal convinces your protagonist's child to commit a heinous crime.
4. Write a scene where a deranged doll tortures one of your protagonist's loved ones. Maybe your protagonist is forced to watch until she agrees to do an illegal and unethical favor for the doll.
5. Your protagonist has been reincarnated as a doll. Write a scene where he cycles through several gnarly emotions about his new state of existence, then causes someone's death (which he has secretly been fantasizing about for years).

PANDORA'S BOX

It's fitting, and a bit unnerving, that the Pandora's Box trope is itself one of the most ancient literary themes. In the story from Greek mythology, Zeus presented Pandora with a box that contained countless evils and instructed her to keep it closed at all costs. Of course, Pandora's curiosity got the better of her. When she opened the box, she released disease, death, and darkness upon the world.

You'd think people would have learned their lesson by now, but the allure of the unknown is invariably too enticing. People always want to know what's inside the box. Which is why this trope is so enduring.

The instant you introduce a sealed container (anything from an ordinary box to a sunken tomb to some kind of enchanted vessel) into your story, with a warning *never* to open it, you're making two promises to your readers: At some point, in a moment of curiosity or foolishness, one of your characters will open that box, and whatever's inside will be dangerous and deadly. The evil in that box has been lying in wait for years, maybe even centuries. It's ready to do some damage.

Now your protagonist must try to rid the world of this evil. But once such deadly forces have been unleashed, it's nearly impossible to contain them. Your protagonist will face grave dangers; make their journey scary enough to give your readers nightmares.

Time's Up

SCENARIO

Your protagonist does something careless that puts the world in mortal danger. Maybe he reads a Latin incantation scribbled in the margins of a vintage tome he finds in his grandmother's attic and awakens a demonic spirit. Or maybe while staying with friends at a rental house for a bachelor party weekend, he drunkenly bashes open a basement door clearly marked "Do Not Open" and unleashes a monster held captive for centuries. Whatever the circumstances, this evil creature now has its sights on your protagonist.

BRAINSTORM

Come up with an origin story for the monster. How long has it been held captive? Who caught it and trapped it here in the first place? Does it have any vendettas? How angry is it? What kind of powers does it possess? Does it appear in corporeal form, or does it manifest itself in more spiritual, psychological, and metaphysical ways? What does it want?

WRITE

Write a frantic scene where your protagonist is pursued through a crowd by the evil spirit or monster. Whenever he asks strangers for help and tries to explain what's happening, people look at him like he's crazy. Your protagonist runs until he reaches a dead end and must face his evil opponent head-on. Is there any way he'll get out of this alive?

Remember: The monster might not want to kill your protagonist. What if it instead wants to use your protagonist in some way? Think of at least five worse-than-death outcomes for the end of this chase sequence.

OPTIONAL ELEMENTS TO INCLUDE

- Oozing pus.
- Your protagonist is alone, but he feels breath on his neck.
- Torrents of blood.

Horror Twist

Sometimes death isn't an ending. Imagine your protagonist is brutally murdered by this evil entity, but his spirit doesn't die. The monster has other ideas for your protagonist; it needs to use him to complete a horrific mission. Think about how it might affect a person's psyche to know they've entered the realm of the undead.

Remember Me?

SCENARIO

They say lightning doesn't strike twice. But what about hidden evils? When your protagonist was younger, she awakened a demon and successfully sealed it away. She thought all that was behind her, but lately she can't shake the feeling that the demon was freed and is watching her. If she's right, can she defeat it a second time?

BRAINSTORM

How many sins has your protagonist committed? Make a list and then rank them from mild to nasty. Which of these sins might she still need to pay for?

WRITE

Your protagonist suspects the evil force that tormented her in the past has been set free to haunt her again. Write a scene where she discovers irrefutable proof. She doesn't want to believe it, but then the demon "speaks" to her through a friend, stranger, pet, or inanimate object. How does it threaten her?

OPTIONAL ELEMENTS TO INCLUDE

- Choking.
- A cut or bruise manifests on her skin.
- Your protagonist loses the ability to speak.

Horror Twist

What if the demon has been here longer than your protagonist realizes? What if he never left? What if he's been watching her for years, waiting for the perfect moment to reappear and drive her mad?

You're Only Making It Worse 

SCENARIO

Your protagonist sets a Cthulhu-like entity free from an old chest inside her home, perhaps in the pantry or a hallway closet, or maybe underneath her child's crib. She's afraid of disturbing the creature and causing it harm, but she thinks it's trying to control her. She is consumed by it, both mentally and emotionally.

BRAINSTORM

Horror writer H.P. Lovecraft created the mythology of Cthulhu, which might be described as an alien monster with tentacles and an octopus-like head that represents the terror of the unknown and various other cosmic horrors. Explore how thinking too much about the vastness of the universe might drive a person insane.

WRITE

Write a scene where your protagonist confides in a friend (or perhaps her therapist) that she has been secretly harboring this ancient monster in her home. How does her confidant react? Do they believe her? What might your protagonist say or do that would make them fear for her safety and for the lives of her loved ones?

Remember: It's possible that this creature is controlling your protagonist, or they might have a symbiotic relationship. If your protagonist senses her friend wants to hurt the monster, she might do something desperate to protect it. What are the ultimate extreme actions she might take?

OPTIONAL ELEMENTS TO INCLUDE

- Blood oozing out of the furniture.
- A strangled moan.
- A door that opens up into a harrowing void.

Horror Twist

As your protagonist's connection to this ancient monster deepens, she begins to lose sight of herself. If the monster wanted her to harm her spouse or her child, would she do it? How far gone is she? What would such an act do to whatever remains of her soul?

Quick Writes

Set a timer for 15 minutes and do not stop writing until the timer goes off. Do not edit, cross out, or censor yourself. Write down every thought that comes to you.

1. Your protagonist's parents die mysteriously. As family members prepare for an estate sale, they discover a locked chest. Write a scene where a minor character breaks the chest open and is brutally attacked by whatever's hiding inside.
2. Your protagonist receives a text with a spam link. Write a scene where he clicks the link and inadvertently summons a demon through his phone. Think about how this demon might use the Internet and Wi-Fi as a means of mass communication.
3. Your pregnant protagonist accidentally releases an ancient demon from a box of vintage children's toys. Write a scene where she expresses a fear that this ancient demon may have altered her unborn child in some inexplicable way.
4. Your protagonist has paid for the deluxe package at a luxurious resort. Write a scene where he is offered an ancient tincture as part of a spa package, and then he inadvertently releases the long-dead evil spirit of one of the hotel's previous inhabitants.
5. Your protagonist is a criminal and thief. Write a scene where he cracks open a safe and releases an ancient evil. Perhaps he is shoved into the safe, where he suddenly finds himself in a terrifying new world.

LEGEND HAS IT

"There's a man with a hook for a hand who lives in those woods. If you bother him, he'll slice you in half. I have a friend who got cut but managed to run away."

"My grandfather is secretly an alien. I saw him without his human skin once. He scared my cousin to death. That's why we never go visit anymore."

"Did you hear about the old lady who lives in that dilapidated house down the street? She eats little kids. Legend Has It you can hear their screams late at night."

Every generation grows up with their own urban myths. Scary stories about awful things that happened in their hometown. These bits of terrifying lore used to get passed around from friend group to friend group, but in the Internet age they go viral and spread farther, mutating in upsetting and dangerous ways. When you hear these stories, you don't want to believe them, but sometimes they sound just realistic enough that you find yourself wondering: *What if it's true?*

Your characters will react in various ways when they hear the words "Legend Has It." Some will proceed with caution; others won't. And the characters who don't believe are usually the ones who meet a bloody fate first. Your readers will take devilish delight in their downfall as they discover the truth they should have believed in all along.

"Take It Back Before It's Too Late"

SCENARIO

Legend has it that an evil entity (maybe the Devil, a witch, or a cannibalistic alien) can be summoned by intoning its name after midnight, reading an incantation found in a rare tome, or repeating a cursed phrase a specific number of times. You decide the various rules and lore that make it possible to bring this creature into the world of your story. And though your protagonist doesn't believe in this old wives' tale, she has enough cautious fear within her that she wouldn't dare do or say anything dumb that might tempt fate.

BRAINSTORM

Think of at least three stories your characters have heard about this evil entity. What details do people often get wrong when sharing scary stories about this legend, and what details do they get right? Come up with a secret power the evil entity possesses that your characters don't know about. How and why is the real thing scarier than the legend?

WRITE

Write a scene where a group of friends are hanging out and, as a joke, one of them casually summons the evil entity. He doesn't think it will work. But your protagonist is superstitious, so when she hears what's happening she begs him to stop. You might try writing the scene a few different ways to see what's more effective: In one version, the entity appears immediately and brutally; in another version, the entity doesn't appear until later that night. In the second version, build the tension slowly. Tease your readers with hints of what's to come.

Remember: Your protagonist has good instincts. If she senses they're in danger, would she stick around to see what happens, or would she make an early exit? Think about what she might do to protect herself and how her intuition might help her survive until the end of your story.

OPTIONAL ELEMENTS TO INCLUDE

- A cracked mirror.
- A mangled limb.
- One of your characters is sucked into an alternate dimension.

Horror Twist

Sometimes the best way to reverse a curse is to give it to someone else. What if one of your protagonist's friends already summoned the evil entity before this scene and he's trying to give the entity a new victim?

Tonight's the Anniversary of When It Happened

SCENARIO

Your protagonist lives in a quiet suburban town. When he was younger, his parents were murdered by a madman who was never caught. Legend has it the murderer still lives in town and may strike again.

BRAINSTORM

Map out what took place on the night of the murder, then come up with five outsized versions of this crime. What details do people get wrong? In what awful ways have people exaggerated what happened? Think about how these rumors affect your protagonist and how they add to the trauma of losing his parents.

WRITE

It's the anniversary of that horrible night. Your protagonist wants to forget what happened, so he goes out for some drunken debauchery. He's in a terrible headspace. Write a scene where he realizes he's being followed.

OPTIONAL ELEMENTS TO INCLUDE

- A stranger accuses your protagonist of being the killer.
- He drunkenly attacks a cop.
- Someone spikes his drink.

Horror Twist

What if your protagonist was home when the murders happened? Maybe he told the police he slept through it, but the awful truth is that he witnessed everything. Those images have played on repeat in his brain ever since, changing him forever.

They Came Here to Study Us

SCENARIO

For decades there have been an abnormally large number of UFO sightings and stories of alien abductions in the small town where your protagonist lives. Legend has it that this isn't an accident. Residents of the area say the government made an agreement with the aliens and sent them here to do testing on humans in exchange for not harming people in the rest of the country, but your protagonist doesn't want to believe this.

BRAINSTORM

Write three testimonials of locals who claim they were abducted. How do their stories differ, and how do their stories perfectly align? Describe their experiences sensually, exploring the sounds, tastes, scents, images, and textures they remember from their alleged time with the aliens.

WRITE

Write a scene where your protagonist tries to debunk the rumors by putting himself in a place where he's vulnerable to a potential abduction. Perhaps he goes into the woods where many of the sightings have occurred, or he camps out on his roof and waits. It starts as a quiet night, but things take a disturbing turn when your protagonist either sees one of his neighbors get abducted or gets abducted himself.

Remember: If your protagonist wasn't a believer before, the events of this night will make him one.

OPTIONAL ELEMENTS TO INCLUDE

- Your protagonist meets his doppelgänger.
- A burning sensation.
- The aliens come from *below* instead of above.

Horror Twist

When your protagonist finally sees alien activity with his own eyes, he might realize that all the other abduction stories he heard were true, including the most horrifying ones. Think about how this knowledge changes him. What extreme actions might he take to avoid the same fate?

Callbacks

What if your protagonist has been abducted before? What if it's happened multiple times but he never remembers it? What if he's a naysayer and doubter because he doesn't want to accept what's happened to him? By denying the truth and pushing it deeper into his subconscious, is he putting anyone else in danger?

Quick Writes

Set a timer for 15 minutes and do not stop writing until the timer goes off. Do not edit, cross out, or censor yourself. Write down every thought that comes to you.

1. According to urban legend, there's a killer who lurks near remote gas stations and will discreetly slash your tires, then offer you a ride. Write a scene where your protagonist reluctantly accepts a ride from a stranger and immediately regrets it.
2. One urban legend warns that you should never flash your lights at a car that doesn't have its headlights on; if you do, the criminals in that car will kidnap you as part of a gang initiation. Write a scene where your protagonist flashes his headlights at another car, then realizes the other car has circled back to follow him.
3. According to urban legend, the Devil himself lives in an abandoned house in your protagonist's neighborhood. Write a scene where your protagonist and a group of friends break in to see if the rumors are true.
4. In one legend, serial killers walk through apartment buildings at night testing doors. If they find one unlocked, they'll go inside and murder the sleeping inhabitants. Write a scene where your protagonist wakes up in the middle of the night to find a stranger staring at her.
5. According to urban legend, your socially awkward teenage protagonist descends from a long line of witches. Write a scene where she decides to prove her tormentors right by treating them to an act of revenge.

CULT OF FEAR

One reason cults hold such power over their followers is that they speak to the primal fear of ending up alone in the world. A cult is like a found family; it provides connection and community, but without all the baggage of the family you grew up with.

Your protagonist will be drawn to a cult because it promises things like community and acceptance. Before you reveal the complicated underbelly of the cult, you will want to capture the feeling that this is a haven where everyone is welcome. Get your readers invested by letting them know why your protagonist wants to be here so badly. Help them believe that if they were in her shoes, they would embrace this place with the same diving-in-head-first gusto. Even if, somewhere deep down, they know there must be brutality hidden behind the façade of perfection.

Unfortunately, your protagonist is going to discover the cult's wickedness—and more. Evil lurks in the shadows here. And everything about the decision to join this cult will soon prove to be disastrously misguided. Your protagonist is in danger. Her new friends are in danger. And it won't be easy to break free. Because once you join a cult, you can't just leave. Not without shedding some blood.

“Don’t Speak Unless You’re Spoken To”

SCENARIO

Your protagonist has been lured into a cult. When she joined, she didn’t understand how strict the rules are, or how poorly the lower-level members are treated. The first time she broke a rule, she didn’t even realize what she’d done. The second time, she was testing the system to see how much she could bend the rules. And the third time, she was deliberately defying them. If she knew how much danger she was in, she wouldn’t have pushed so hard.

BRAINSTORM

Come up with a set of rules everyone in this cult must follow. What privileges can be earned, and what are the punishments for breaking the rules? If the cult has a caste system, describe the hierarchical levels between a newbie and the leader.

WRITE

Your protagonist does something so simple she assumed she didn’t need permission. Maybe she makes casual conversation with an upper-level member of the cult, or maybe she uses a bathroom reserved for members with higher status. She is swiftly punished. Write a scene where an upper-level member takes her to a private room and teaches her a lesson in subservience.

Remember: Your protagonist might mostly do what she’s told, but she has a defiant streak, so find a moment where she stands up for herself.

OPTIONAL ELEMENTS TO INCLUDE

- A common household item used as a weapon.
- She is forced into an act of humiliation, like licking the floor.
- She discreetly steals a personal item that doesn’t belong to her.

Horror Twist

What if the social hierarchy of this cult is fake? What if it's impossible to rise in the ranks and the subservient members will always be treated like slaves? The rules teach lowly members not to fight back. What ulterior motives might the cult leaders have? What if they have sinister plans for their lowliest members? Your protagonist has no idea what horrors await her.

Put This On

SCENARIO

Your protagonist is part of a cult that doesn't believe in self-expression. Members wear cloaks when they're together, their faces hidden and shrouded in mystery. Anything that brings attention to a person's individuality is considered a sin. Artistry? Sin. Sense of humor? Sin. Empathy? The biggest sin of all. Your protagonist doesn't believe in this place anymore. He has begun making plans to leave, something he's only confided to a few select people—the people he trusts most.

BRAINSTORM

Your protagonist didn't make this decision lightly. He's been planning his escape for months. Figure out how he intends to sneak off in the middle of the night. How would his plan unfold if everything went perfectly? What are the various ways his escape could go wrong?

WRITE

Write a scene where your protagonist is awakened in the middle of the night by a man who puts a sack over his head. The man takes your protagonist into custody. Your protagonist soon finds himself in a room surrounded by fellow cult members. They found out about his plan, and they must inflict punishment. Your protagonist's pain will be tonight's entertainment.

Remember: These people usually hide their faces behind cloaks, so your protagonist may not even know what many of his friends look like, but he knows their voices. Which means he will still know who's cheering as he is violently beaten.

OPTIONAL ELEMENTS TO INCLUDE

- A rabid dog.
- Chains.
- Your protagonist is branded with a hot iron.

Horror Twist

What if the cult makes extra income by livestreaming punishment ceremonies on the dark web? Your protagonist's punishment is tonight's featured entertainment. And the audience loves what they see.

Take Me—I'm Ready

SCENARIO

Your protagonist was born in a cult. He grew up believing what he was told, anything from "enlightenment is gained through subservience" to "human sacrifice is required to appease the angry gods." But lately he has begun to question these beliefs. He'll be punished if anyone finds out he disagrees with them, so he stays silent.

BRAINSTORM

This cult has a set of commandments that members are told came from a divine source. Come up with at least ten rules cult members must follow. Why did the original cult leaders select these rules? How do they benefit those at the top?

WRITE

Write a scene where your protagonist finds out his parents are going to offer themselves up as human sacrifices. They believe they are doing this for the common good, but your protagonist sees how they've been manipulated. He tries to get them to change their minds.

OPTIONAL ELEMENTS TO INCLUDE

- Your protagonist offers to sacrifice himself instead.
- Spiders.
- An ablution ritual.

Horror Twist

Why do the cult leaders need human sacrifice? Is it an act of control? What if it's for more utilitarian reasons? Maybe their meat rations are low and they need members to provide for each other. How does your protagonist stop his parents?

Quick Writes

Set a timer for 15 minutes and do not stop writing until the timer goes off. Do not edit, cross out, or censor yourself. Write down every thought that comes to you.

1. Your protagonist finally escaped the cult she was trapped in for years, but they keep trying to pull her back in. Write a scene where several members of her former cult confront her at her day job and make trouble.
2. Your protagonist is an undercover cop, a journalist, or a parent who has infiltrated a cult to find his brainwashed child. Write a scene where the cult leader asks him to perform an act of sacrifice to prove his loyalty to the group.
3. Write a scene leading up to an elaborate ritual ceremony, write the ceremony itself, and write the aftermath of the ceremony. Explore this sequence from the perspective of a character who's feeling disillusioned by the cult and desperately wants out.
4. Write a late-night orgy scene involving several members of a doomsday cult. When they wake up the next day to discover the world isn't over, one member of the group violently turns on the others.
5. Write an initiation scene where your protagonist is indoctrinated into her new cult. As several cultists break her down emotionally, she has second thoughts about joining. But there's no way out.

CAME BACK WRONG

Death is supposed to be a final destination—not a vacation you come home from.

But when one of your characters messes with the natural order of things and attempts to bring a loved one back to life, things are bound to go badly. Odds are they will discover their loved one Came Back Wrong.

You might argue that having your loved one back in any form is better than not having them at all, but you're wrong; no one wants them back like this. Even if your protagonist tries to pretend their loved one's return is a good thing, they won't believe that for long. They'll quickly discover the return puts their own life at risk.

A loved one's resurrection could go wrong in so many ways. Maybe they've been possessed by a bloodthirsty demonic spirit, or their body is literally falling apart, or their brain is fried and they've been transformed into a raving psychopath.

The tragic arc of Came Back Wrong stories is that your protagonist ultimately must reverse the resurrection. If he wants to live, that is. He'll have to send his loved one back to the other side. And losing them a second time will be even more painful than before, because this time he knows it's real. This time he understands there's no coming back.

"Mom, Is That You?"

SCENARIO

Your protagonist is still reeling from the unexpected and untimely death of her mother (or you can swap in a spouse, child, or any other family member/close companion). They had a difficult relationship, with many unresolved issues. Their relationship was so fraught that your protagonist is determined to find a sense of closure. She will do anything to get one more chance to communicate with her dead loved one.

BRAINSTORM

Why was their relationship so strained? Make a quick list of harmful things your protagonist's mom did and said to her over the years. Then look at things from the mother's perspective: Did she feel hurt and abused by your protagonist? Did they both inflict pain on each other? Or does one of them feel gaslit/wronged by the other? What did they fight about? Get into both of their heads.

WRITE

Write a scene where your protagonist performs an elaborate ceremony to temporarily bring her mother back from the dead. She gets something wrong and accidentally brings her mother back in an altered state. Instead of getting the closure she wants, she has opened herself up to a sickening, scary new chapter in their relationship. Nothing about this is going to be good or easy.

Remember: This isn't your protagonist's mother. Not really. Think about how death may have changed her physically, emotionally, and spiritually. How much danger is your protagonist putting herself in by bringing her mom back? Make this a bloody family reunion.

OPTIONAL ELEMENTS TO INCLUDE

- A twisted memory.
- An accusation.
- An emotional wound that manifests in physical form.

Horror Twist

Who does your protagonist go to for help bringing her mother back from the dead? What ulterior motives might this other character have? Maybe they intentionally messed up the resurrection to hurt your protagonist. Explore the potentially deadly consequences of this action.

Callbacks

Think about your protagonist's final interaction with her mother. What were her mother's last words? Have her echo those words in this scene, but with a new meaning.

“It Isn’t Safe Here”

SCENARIO

Your protagonist is taking care of a resurrected loved one who doesn’t appear to have changed at all. If you didn’t know they’d been dead for several weeks (or months), then you’d probably assume they’re just in an antisocial mood. Until you look them in the eyes, that is. There’s something in their eyes that’s off. A malicious glimmer. You might even call it a hunger.

BRAINSTORM

Before the loved one died, what was their daily routine? What were their interests, their hopes, their dreams? Think about the things your protagonist must do to try to make things appear normal again. But nothing goes right. What does your protagonist tell himself to convince himself this could work?

WRITE

Write a series of scenes where your protagonist attempts to do casual, everyday activities with his resurrected loved one but his loved one gets increasingly agitated. At one point, someone calls your protagonist out and warns him that he’s playing with fire. The resurrected loved one seems coiled for attack—it’s like they’re vibrating with violence—but your protagonist still doesn’t want to see the danger right in front of his eyes.

Remember: The easiest person to lie to is yourself. Is there a moment when your protagonist finally realizes how much danger he’s in? Make it feel like all the walls around him are crashing down. What madness has he gotten himself into?

OPTIONAL ELEMENTS TO INCLUDE

- Bugs crawl out of one of the dead loved one’s orifices.
- A message from the other side.
- Whimpering.

Horror Twist

Think about how your protagonist's loved one may have been physically transformed in death. What if they possess superhuman strength and an animalistic brutality? What if their skin looks normal but crinkles and sheds when touched? What if they have a toxic smell?

Callbacks

Write a quick, rough version of an earlier scene between these two characters when life was good. What was the best moment they ever spent together? Make your readers feel the absence of this once-great connection.

“Sometimes I Wish I Was One of Them”

SCENARIO

Your protagonist has been through so much death that she is in a constant state of mourning. It’s difficult to feel connected to daily life when so many people she cares about are gone. Every night she has nightmares about them coming back to life.

BRAINSTORM

Your protagonist has lost five or more people she’s close to. Name them, and quickly freewrite about what your protagonist misses most about each one. Would she kill to bring them back to life? Is she capable of that?

WRITE

Write a scene where your protagonist vents to a therapist or doctor (or perhaps a witch or shaman) about all the loss she has suffered. Instead of giving her advice, this person she’s confiding in says he has an answer: “I can help you bring them back.”

OPTIONAL ELEMENTS TO INCLUDE

- An article of clothing that belongs to a lost loved one.
- A pricked finger.
- An ignored warning.

Horror Twist

Your protagonist feels depressed, sad, alone. But does she also feel a little bit of guilt? What if she’s responsible for the death of one of her loved ones? Maybe that’s why she keeps having nightmares—she can’t stop seeing his blood on her hands.

Quick Writes

Set a timer for 15 minutes and do not stop writing until the timer goes off. Do not edit, cross out, or censor yourself. Write down every thought that comes to you.

1. Your protagonist's resurrected loved one has a message from the beyond: "Death is coming for you." Turns out you can't bring someone back without consequences. Write a scene where your protagonist makes a desperate attempt to flee death.
2. Write a scene where your protagonist attempts to resurrect a lost loved one at a cemetery, but he accidentally resurrects the wrong corpse—or maybe a few of them.
3. Your protagonist's resurrected loved one hasn't said a word since she came back; write a scene where your protagonist discovers the loved one doing something animalistic (like hunting and eating a rat). How does your protagonist try to fix them?
4. Your protagonist's resurrected loved one has a craving for human flesh. Write a scene where he tries to convince your protagonist to kill for him.
5. Your protagonist's resurrected loved one is falling apart, literally. The loved one's body is a rotten mess. Write a scene where your protagonist takes his loved one to a plastic surgeon, who turns them away. This makes the loved one angry . . .

EVIL OBJECTS

Sometimes the deepest scare can be found in the most mundane place. In an everyday object, for instance. Imagine your characters are gathered around the dining table for Sunday dinner when the carving knife launches itself into your protagonist's hand and compels her (against her will) to stab her abusive brother in the neck. For an instant, she felt like she was possessed by the knife!

Or imagine the compact in your protagonist's purse contains her shadow self. Whenever she looks at it, her reflection berates her to the point that she will do *anything* to feel normal again. She feels cursed every time she looks at the handheld mirror.

Or imagine your protagonist buys a ring at a yard sale and wearing it makes her feel the pain of all the women who owned this ring in the past. She feels haunted by the previous ring owners, and now she's bloodthirsty for justice.

Evil Objects most commonly fall into one of three categories: Cursed, Possessed, and Haunted. Cursed Objects will bring bad luck upon their owners or cause them to do harmful things. A Possessed Object is controlled by demonic spirits and will inflict harm on others (or force its bearer to inflict harm). And Haunted Objects contain the souls of the dead and can form spiritual connections with those who touch them. All Evil Objects can serve as exciting wild cards to throw into your story, so pick an object and transform it into an instrument of evil—the more wicked the better.

Don't Go Near That

SCENARIO

Your protagonist is visiting an elderly family member, helping them sort through storage or downsize their home to prepare for a big move. He's always been a little creeped out by this family member; there's just something *not quite right* about her. But she's blood, so what are you gonna do? Little does he know, he's about to discover an object in her home that might explain why she's always been *off*. This object is about to change his life in a terrible way.

BRAINSTORM

Think about this black-sheep member of your protagonist's family. What stories do people tell when they're talking about her behind her back? How does she behave at family gatherings? Has she ever made off-color comments that didn't sit well with your protagonist? Has she ever done or said something that makes others incredibly uncomfortable? Why do people fear her? Once you've come up with some of her lore, find a way to connect her behavior to this Evil Object she has tucked away at home—this object she can't seem to get rid of.

WRITE

Write a scene where your protagonist opens a box, chest, or trunk that doesn't seem out of the ordinary in any way. No need to even bother donating most of this stuff; it can go straight into the junk pile. But one object in the box draws his attention; perhaps he's drawn to it because it's *cursed*. When his family member sees him holding this object, she goes ballistic.

Remember: This cursed object has belonged to the family member for a long time. Is it possible for her to give it to your protagonist? Could this entire visit be a setup or a trap?

OPTIONAL ELEMENTS TO INCLUDE

- Insane laughter.
- A rusty key.
- The object forms a psychic connection with whoever touches it.

Horror Twist

Think about the object's powers. What does the object want? The object has a lot of freaky, dangerous desires. What if the keeper of this object is forced to do its bidding?

Callbacks

Can your protagonist remember a time when his family member wasn't such a scary outsider? If this Evil Object made her into the person she is today, will it do the same to him?

I Haven't Seen One of These in Years

SCENARIO

Modern technology is constantly evolving. The most expensive piece of tech you own might be obsolete a year from now. Does an object know its value? Can an object inflict pain?

BRAINSTORM

Make a list of items you've owned (or that an older generation owned) that are outdated (a VCR, typewriter, flip phone, etc.). If each of these objects could think and feel, what would they be most proud of? What would they fear?

WRITE

Your protagonist acts carelessly around an older stranger (perhaps a new neighbor, someone who works in the same office building, or a service worker) by either not including them in a group or overlooking them in some way. This person is tired of feeling unseen, so they put a spell on a similarly ignored object in your protagonist's home. Write a scene where an outdated piece of technology at the bottom of your protagonist's closet is possessed by this angry stranger. And it's out for blood.

OPTIONAL ELEMENTS TO INCLUDE

- A rotten stench.
- A string of curse words.
- A leaking fluid.

Horror Twist

What if the possessed object can infect other forgotten pieces of technology in your protagonist's home? How would your protagonist react if he discovered the possessed objects in his home were forming an army?

“I Told You to Get Rid of It”

SCENARIO

Your protagonist discovers an ancient artifact while on vacation and brings it home with him. He's drawn to this object in a way he doesn't understand. He feels as if the object is calling to him, as if it's demanding his attention. It gets so bad that other people in his life call him out on it, expressing worry about him and fear that he's becoming distant. But the more they try to get him to change, the more he alienates those closest to him.

BRAINSTORM

Is this haunted artifact alive? Is it being controlled by an ancient evil in another dimension? Think about the sinister secrets it holds and all the different ways this object might communicate with your protagonist. Is there a reason it was drawn to your protagonist, or was it just a case of bad luck that he happened to find the haunted object? Was he just the wrong person at the wrong time?

WRITE

Write a scene where your protagonist tries to get rid of the object by either destroying it, dumping it somewhere, or giving it away. He knows this haunted object is bad for him, even though he doesn't understand why. But no matter how hard he tries to get rid of it, he can't; his desperation is building.

Remember: It's up to you to decide what evil powers this object holds. What if your protagonist mistakenly thinks the object is a source of good at first, and he doesn't realize its true evil intentions until it's too late for him to do anything to stop it?

OPTIONAL ELEMENTS TO INCLUDE

- Your protagonist consumes the artifact.
- Your protagonist caresses the artifact.
- Your protagonist uses the artifact as a weapon.

Horror Twist

What if the haunted object and your protagonist are linked and every time he tries to destroy, break, or hurt it, he only ends up causing himself pain? What terrible procedure must he undergo to separate himself from this object he's inextricably connected to?

Callbacks

Think about the moment your protagonist found this object. Can you hint at the danger to come when you first describe it? What warnings would it potentially give off?

Quick Writes

Set a timer for 15 minutes and do not stop writing until the timer goes off. Do not edit, cross out, or censor yourself. Write down every thought that comes to you.

1. Write a scene where your protagonist finds a haunted weapon (anything from an antique sword to a rusty knife) and senses the dangerous object is communicating with her. She feels as if the weapon is giving her orders to fulfill its desires.
2. A distant relative unexpectedly shows up at your protagonist's home with a gift. Write a scene where this relative seems a little too eager to give away this mysterious object (spoiler: It's cursed), demanding that your protagonist take it off their hands.
3. Your protagonist finds an unusual toy at a yard sale and buys it for her niece, nephew, or child. Write a scene where the possessed toy attacks the family pet or a nosy neighbor. Is it protecting your protagonist's family, or will it hurt them too?
4. Write a scene where a possessed appliance communicates with one of your characters and convinces him to commit an act of violence against a total stranger.
5. Your protagonist is on vacation with either her family or a group of friends. They've heard rumors that their hotel is haunted. Write a scene where someone in the group gets attacked by a haunted item on the room service tray.

BITTEN

Transformation is at the root of most great stories, particularly in the horror genre. And being Bitten forces your protagonist to change in the most unpredictable ways. All your readers know for sure is: This won't end well. Here are a few possible scenarios:

- **Zombie:** Any character Bitten by the undead is destined to join them. The big question is: How many people will he endanger before he succumbs?
- **Werewolf:** Your protagonist is attacked by what appears to be a wild animal, but it's really part man, part beast, and now your protagonist is one of them too—cursed to follow his basest instincts every time he morphs into his new monstrous form.
- **Vampire:** Your protagonist is lured into the seductive arms of a vampire, who hungrily bites his neck and drains the life out of him, transforming him into an eternal nightwalker, a predator who must feed on others weaker than him to survive.

A bite doesn't have to be supernatural to be scary. The bite of a rabid dog or a sadistic child could lead your protagonist down an equally horrific path. No matter what kind of bite it is, make sure your readers understand what's at stake for your protagonist. If they know what being Bitten stole from him, they'll feel his pain, and they'll be dying to see if he can find a way back to his better self.

Lift Your Shirt—Show Me 

SCENARIO

Your protagonist is part of a group of weary travelers looking for safety. They've survived some sort of apocalyptic event. A virus has ravaged half the population, turning the masses into flesh-eating creatures. Your protagonist wants safety, a good meal, and human connection. The only thing keeping him going is the possibility that one of his loved ones is still out there somewhere and he'll be able to find her. He spends every moment hoping and praying she's still alive.

BRAINSTORM

Jot down several dates: Ten Days After the Apocalypse, Twenty Days After, Fifty Days After, and so on. Then chart your protagonist's headspace at each of these points in his journey and how his emotions have evolved. How is he able to keep his loved one(s) present in his memories? Does he tell stories about them to the others in his group, or does he keep his thoughts to himself? Think of at least two interactions he's had with strangers that have convinced him not to give up his search.

WRITE

The group occasionally encounters undead creatures on their journey. Write a scene where another member of the group discovers your protagonist was Bitten during one of these interactions. He's been hiding this wound from everyone because he doesn't want them to abandon him—or worse. Many members of the group would kill him if they knew he'd been Bitten. Can he talk his way out of that fate now?

Remember: Every zombie story is different. You get to set the parameters for the world of your story. Does a bite guarantee transformation? Or is it possible to heal from some bites before you become one of *them*? Come up with your own rules and stick to them.

OPTIONAL ELEMENTS TO INCLUDE

- A hallucination.
- The group is interrupted by an attacking zombie.
- Gunfire.

Horror Twist

Quickly jot down everything you know about zombies. Think about your favorite zombie stories. How do people become zombies, how do zombies behave, and how are zombies killed? How can you twist the zombie genre to make it feel fresh and surprising again—or, to put it more bluntly, how can you bring this genre back to life? What is your version of the ultimate deadly zombie?

How Long Ago Did It Happen?

SCENARIO

Your protagonist has a secret. When he was younger, a werewolf bit him. Only a few people know about his deadly double life, and he always maintains that he can't remember his extracurricular lupine activities. However, he remembers every second of his uncontrollable, animalistic adventures. He's haunted by the things he's done.

BRAINSTORM

Your protagonist is two different people: He has a human self and an animal self. Each of these selves has a different way of thinking, behaving, and communicating. Write an inner monologue for each of his selves during a moment of intense excitement.

WRITE

Write a scene where your protagonist decides to confide in someone he trusts about his secret double life but his revelation does not go over well. By the end of the scene, his "trusted" confidant is unconscious, incapacitated, or dead. Or maybe the scene builds to a moment when the confidant is Bitten.

OPTIONAL ELEMENTS TO INCLUDE

- A moment of extreme agitation.
- A frantic phone call.
- A plea for forgiveness.

Horror Twist

If your protagonist ends up biting his confidant, think about all the ways this could go wrong. What if they don't become a werewolf but instead morph into something much worse?

You'll Get Us All Killed

SCENARIO

A group of friends are trapped in a dark, damp place—anywhere from a mausoleum to a hidden bunker to a secret underground tunnel. They've locked themselves in here to get away from a danger lurking outside. They have no idea that their "safe" hiding spot is actually a nest.

BRAINSTORM

Your protagonist and his friends don't know how many hiding places there are here. Map out the geography of this location and come up with at least four spaces where villainous people, creatures, or monsters could be lying in wait for them.

WRITE

Your protagonist sees or hears something that freaks him out. His instincts tell him they aren't as safe as they thought they were and maybe they'd be better off outside. But before he can escape, another member of the group stops him. Write a scene where the group gets into an intense fight/debate about their best course of action: Should they stay or should they go?

Remember: They aren't alone. And the longer they argue, the more likely it is that one of them will get hurt. Build the scene to a crescendo of chaos as a member of the group gets Bitten and the verbal fight turns into a physical one.

OPTIONAL ELEMENTS TO INCLUDE

- A toxic stench.
- Laughter coming from the shadows.
- One member of the group is torn limb from limb.

Horror Twist

Your protagonist senses something is wrong. What if his instincts have been telling him that for a while? Consider the idea that one of his friends is working with the creatures who are nesting here. Maybe they didn't choose this hiding place randomly or by accident—what if they were lured here? The whole thing was a trap. But will your protagonist realize this in time to get out alive? And how many of his friends will he be able to save?

Quick Writes

Set a timer for 15 minutes and do not stop writing until the timer goes off. Do not edit, cross out, or censor yourself. Write down every thought that comes to you.

1. Write a scene where your protagonist is Bitten by an unusual animal and the wound begins to take over his entire body, morphing and mutating until your protagonist becomes an unrecognizable monster.
2. Your protagonist was Bitten in the middle of the night, and ever since then he's felt odd. Write a scene where he hears his wound talking. The wound has taken control of him, and it wants him to do terrible things.
3. Your protagonist wants to get Bitten. Write a seduction scene where she tries to coerce a vampire, werewolf, or other supernatural creature to "turn" her but the supernatural character doesn't think she's ready.
4. Write a scene where your protagonist is on a date with a cannibal but she doesn't know it. He is desperate for a bite of her flesh. Build the tension as he looks for the right moment to make his move.
5. Your protagonist is a zombie who hates the taste of flesh. Write a scene where he struggles with the urge to hunt down a victim and then finally succumbs to his base instincts out of necessity.

TORTURED

Why would anyone want to read a story in which characters go through terrible traumas?

Some people find a perverse pleasure in the suffering of others. A thrill, almost. As a character is physically and emotionally destroyed, readers can always remind themselves: *At least it's not me.* They can distance themselves from their real fears as they read about the dangers facing their fictional friends.

That doesn't mean stories about Tortured characters are ever an easy read. Readers might require an "every light in the house must be on even though it's midnight" reading experience, plowing forward into the next chapter, feeling both terrified and curious about how much more their favorite character must endure. As much as they might want to stop reading, they still need to get to the end to find out if this Tortured character will survive.

Just be aware that stories of abuse and torture can be a bridge too far for some readers. As you launch into writing your traumatic tale of physical abuse, you might lose some people. But think about it this way: Knowing that some readers may not make it to the end can free you to share even more grim and gory details with those brave enough to keep reading.

Please Let Me Go

SCENARIO

Your protagonist had a strictly religious upbringing. Now that she's older, she has begun to question her faith and has decided to leave the church. Maybe she's been vocal about the new path she plans to explore, or maybe she has just one close confidant. Either way, word has gotten around. People are upset. And then, late one night, she is awakened by the sounds of people coming into her room. Before she can react, several masked intruders attack. They put a pillowcase over her head and abduct her.

BRAINSTORM

Think through your protagonist's journey with faith and a higher power. How were her early beliefs formed, and when/where/why did she begin to see cracks in the façade of religion? Was there a tipping point—a specific moment where she realized she needed a clean break? Or did it happen gradually? Write the words "I believe" and then complete that statement with monologues written in your protagonist's voice at three different points in her life.

WRITE

Your protagonist is being held captive. You decide what her relationship is with her attackers and whether they keep their masks on or not. Write a scene where she is put through a form of medieval torture. When she begs them to stop, she isn't just talking to her attackers—she's talking to her higher power, as well.

Remember: You have a few different directions you can go with your attackers. They might be ordinary humans—perhaps family members—who are so blinded by faith they can't stand the thought of one of their own leaving the fold. Or they might be human vessels controlled by Satan, demons, or any other angry higher power.

OPTIONAL ELEMENTS TO INCLUDE

- A bleeding crucifix.
- Rats, cockroaches, and other vermin.
- A deal with the Devil.

Horror Twist

What if the human villains of your story are serving an evil overlord of an entirely different kind? They might worship an unseen cosmic force they believe is destined to defeat humanity, saving only the clean and pure. In that case, they might perform their torturous deeds as acts of ablution, believing they are helping your protagonist survive the end of the world as we know it.

You Did This to Yourself

SCENARIO

Your protagonist works at a high-end resort. She doesn't have clearance for some of the VIP areas, but she's curious about what their elite members spend so much money on. So, one night she sneaks into a restricted area. And she's horrified by what she sees.

BRAINSTORM

Your protagonist can't afford to lose this job—it pays well and provides benefits. But she also has a good heart and believes in doing the right thing. Do some freewriting to describe her emotional and financial obligations. Determine what's at stake for her if she attracts the attention of the elite.

WRITE

Write a scene where your protagonist accidentally witnesses a wealthy stranger beating up one of her coworkers. The coworker doesn't fight back. Your protagonist realizes the coworker has submitted herself to this man as a resort "service" or perk.

OPTIONAL ELEMENTS TO INCLUDE

- Whips and chains.
- A baptism.
- The coworker is forced to crawl on all fours and bark.

Horror Twist

As your protagonist digs deeper into what's going on, she might discover some startling secrets about the people who originally built this resort. What if she discovers they believed in Satan and the occult?

You Can Choose to Feel Better

SCENARIO

Your protagonist is ready to move on from a professional relationship—anyone from his therapist to his accountant to his personal trainer. He's been with this person for a long time, but there's something about the way she's been talking to him lately that rubs him the wrong way. He can't quite put his finger on it, but there's something off about her.

BRAINSTORM

Make a list of warning signs your protagonist has been privately clocking that led to this decision. How much does he know about this person's personal life? Are there any red flags he missed? Has he talked to any friends about this person and how uncomfortable she makes him? If he suddenly went missing, who would be the first person to notice, and how long would it take them to realize something's wrong?

WRITE

Write a scene where your protagonist tries to break things off but this woman doesn't want to sever their professional relationship. In fact, she won't let him leave now—or ever. Not if he's going to be so "dumb" as to think he doesn't need her anymore. And she has ways of making him change his mind—means of torture to punish him for even thinking of moving on.

Remember: If this breakup scene takes place in the antagonist's office, does that mean there are other people nearby—people your protagonist might be able to reach out to for help? Or does the antagonist have soundproofed doors, or even a hidden/private torture chamber? Think about the geography of her office space and how it can amplify the terror of this situation.

OPTIONAL ELEMENTS TO INCLUDE

- Your protagonist slits the antagonist's throat, but she doesn't die.
- The antagonist speaks in tongues.
- A demon is wearing the antagonist's body as a suit.

Horror Twist

A professional relationship with a service provider requires a lot of give-and-take. What if the antagonist has been taking things from your protagonist without his ever realizing it? Perhaps she can literally eat a person's emotions. The more she tortures him, the stronger she gets.

Quick Writes

Set a timer for 15 minutes and do not stop writing until the timer goes off. Do not edit, cross out, or censor yourself. Write down every thought that comes to you.

1. Your protagonist was trafficked, tortured, and killed. But death doesn't disturb her. Write a scene where she decides to haunt her killer and stop him from torturing anyone else.
2. Your protagonist is stranded on a remote island. But he's not alone. Write a scene where the other inhabitant of this island tortures your protagonist to teach him a lesson: *This land does not belong to you.*
3. Your protagonist is on vacation at a private resort. Write a scene where he is drugged by an employee and wakes up in a torture chamber. Turns out he's been sold to a resort VIP who needs to let off some steam and release some anger.
4. Write a scene where your protagonist goes in for dental work, and after the dentist administers the nitrous oxide, he pulls out the heavy-duty tools. Your protagonist is losing more than just a tooth today.
5. Write a revenge scene. Your protagonist lost a loved one at the hands of a maniac, but now he has the upper hand. He has captured the killer. And he's going to make sure this man feels his pain.

THEY'RE LIVING IN THE WALLS

If these walls could talk, they would scare you to death. That's because they hold deep, dark secrets. Not the kind of secrets you gossip about with friends—no, these secrets are more tangible. These are secrets you can touch. Or, more specifically, secrets that can touch you. Because They're Living in the Walls.

Your protagonist has no idea. There might be subtle hints at first that she misses. An unusual sound in the middle of the night. Some food missing from the pantry. A lost sweater. A piece of furniture that's slightly askew.

But she doesn't pay attention. She's too busy going about her routine. Getting the kids to school. Clocking into her remote job. Doing laundry and other chores. Preparing dinner for the kids while getting ready for a date before the sitter arrives. All the minutiae of a life. She doesn't have time to worry about serial killers, maniacs, monsters, and other vague threats posed by the outside world. But she'd be terrified if she knew how close they were.

You might let your readers in on the house's secret before your protagonist finds out. Keep them on the edge of their seats as they anticipate the moment when she discovers she isn't alone and her whole world turns upside down. Or maybe you withhold the truth from your readers too and let them find out with your protagonist. Either way, this trope will keep your readers on edge as they wonder what might be living in *their* walls.

"I Swear That Wasn't There Before"

SCENARIO

Your protagonist lives alone. He isn't expecting visitors today. No one has a key to his place. There's no reason for his belongings to move, or for a personal item to go missing. His entire home should be as he left it this morning. And yet he's about to discover something amiss.

BRAINSTORM

Do a mental sketch of your protagonist's home and map out all the potential hiding places, both the obvious ones and the ones that might require a little digging—perhaps even literal digging. How well does he know his home? Aside from the stranger(s) hiding within the walls, what other secrets might this home hold?

WRITE

Write a scene where your protagonist brings a date home. They have a few drinks, they flirt, they kiss. The vibes are light and fun. As their connection escalates, they move things into the bedroom—and that's when your protagonist stops dead in his tracks. Because there is an ominous box sitting on his bed. A gift, perhaps, wrapped in butcher paper. Whatever it is, it wasn't there before. Which means someone's been in this room—and they might still be here.

Remember: Your protagonist is going to have to open this box, no matter how scary it might seem. What's the most horrifying reveal you can think of? Brainstorm thirty possible things he might find, getting more gruesome as you go.

OPTIONAL ELEMENTS TO INCLUDE

- Mice.
- Blood (or another foul fluid) dripping from the ceiling.
- Whatever's inside the box is alive.

Horror Twist

What if the gift is a misdirect? What if your protagonist's date *is* the monster living inside his walls, and now that they've shared this scare together it's bonded them? He trusts this person. If only he knew they've been watching him for months—watching him eat, sleep, shower, get dressed. Your protagonist is falling into the arms of a monster, and he has absolutely no idea.

Shhhh, Listen

SCENARIO

Your protagonist is often the first to arrive at the office and the last to leave. Sometimes he works so late he ends up sleeping there. He has no idea this office was built over a portal to a hellish dimension. Every night when the door opens, creatures come through.

BRAINSTORM

Close your eyes. Listen to the gentle buzz of the air conditioner, the chirping of the birds outside, the scuffing sounds of someone walking down the hall. What if there were unexpected sounds coming from the vents too, or heavy breathing? What would you do?

WRITE

It's late at night. Write a scene where your protagonist goes into the office kitchen to brew coffee and discovers several creatures eating from the communal snack tray. These creatures have sharp fangs. As soon as they see your protagonist, they recognize him as a much more enticing snack.

OPTIONAL ELEMENTS TO INCLUDE

- A frantic chase through several corridors.
- A nest.
- A moment of physical transformation.

Horror Twist

Think about how many of these creatures might be hiding within the walls of this office building. Your protagonist might be able to fight off one creature, but what about five? Ten? Thirty?

Someone's Sleeping in My Bed

SCENARIO

Your protagonist was recently evicted, but he knows about a secret attic in his childhood home. So, he discreetly sneaks into his old house and moves into the attic, even though the home is currently occupied. He's the one Living in the Walls, but here's the twist: The current owners of this home are the last people you would ever want to live with. Think dangerous psychopaths.

BRAINSTORM

Do some freewriting about the current owners of your protagonist's childhood home. Come up with at least ten terrible things they've done—anything from murder to kidnapping to torture. If your protagonist knew any of their backstory, he never would have decided to squat here. He'll be lucky if he gets out of his hiding space alive.

WRITE

Your protagonist thinks he's home alone, but he's mistaken. Write a scene where he ventures out of his hiding space to do some snooping around the house. He doesn't yet know how bad these people are, but maybe he finds something in this scene that gives him some insight into their past misdeeds. Before he can change his mind and leave, he hears a voice and must retreat into his hiding spot.

OPTIONAL ELEMENTS TO INCLUDE

- A bloody dish towel.
- A diary filled with Satanic ravings.
- Handcuffs.

Horror Twist

You might think of this as a horror twist on the story of Goldilocks and the Three Bears. Your protagonist has entered a space where he doesn't belong, but that doesn't mean he's the bad guy. There are people living within these walls who could rip him to shreds if they wanted to.

Callbacks

Your protagonist lived here when he was a child, and he probably used to hide in this secret room. Does he find anything from his childhood that's still here after all these years? Perhaps he discovers an object he could use as a weapon for self-defense later in your story.

Quick Writes

Set a timer for 15 minutes and do not stop writing until the timer goes off. Do not edit, cross out, or censor yourself. Write down every thought that comes to you.

1. Write a scene where your protagonist wakes up to find a monster (either humanoid or creature) emerging through some slats in his bedroom floor. The monster is blocking the exit, so your protagonist will have to improvise a weapon if he wants to get out.
2. Your protagonist has a vermin problem. Write a scene where she's setting up some traps and discovers a secret door that leads to a hidden room. When she tries to retreat, she discovers she's locked inside. Where does she go from here?
3. Ever since discovering his home was the site of a murder-suicide, your protagonist has become obsessed with true crime podcasts and unsolved mysteries. He is convinced that the ghosts of the home's former occupants are still living within his walls. Write a scene where he confronts these ghosts.
4. Your protagonist has just arrived home after a long vacation. Write a scene where a neighbor sends her a text message complaining about her creepy house sitter. There's only one problem: Your protagonist never hired a house sitter.
5. Write a scene where your protagonist goes down to her basement. She's getting ready to carry some firewood up the stairs when she hears a click—someone has locked the basement door from the other side. She hears a voice say, "I live here now." What does your protagonist do next?

SERIAL KILLER

John Wayne Gacy. Ted Bundy. Jeffrey Dahmer. The Boston Strangler. Aileen Wuornos. There are terrifying real-life monsters who live relatively normal lives, going about their daily errands just like everybody else.

One of your neighbors might be a serial killer. Or one of the people you trust with your life, like your doctor or your therapist, might also be in the business of murdering people after hours. You might even have a killer in your family. The terrifying truth is you never know what kind of nasty trouble a person gets into in their spare time.

There are two ways to tackle a Serial Killer story. You can write from the point of view of either the killer or one of his potential victims. Either way, you'll want to think about why your antagonist has a desire to kill. Does he have a God complex and commit his crimes to rid the world of evil? Does he get a perverse thrill out of killing because it satisfies a deep, forbidden lust—a hunger he's desperate to feed? Was he abused as a child? Have years of trauma caused him to feel like a victim and crave control? Or was he born like this—a disastrous anomaly of genetics?

Writing a Serial Killer story allows you to explore the nature of evil. Delve deeply into the serial killer's psyche so your readers understand what a truly harrowing situation your protagonist faces.

"I'll Always Keep a Piece of You with Me"

SCENARIO

I should have listened to my instincts. That's what your protagonist keeps telling herself, ever since that man asked her for help lifting a piece of furniture into the back of his van. He seemed so nice. But there was a little voice in the back of her head that said *Run.* If only she had listened, maybe she wouldn't be bound and gagged in his basement now.

BRAINSTORM

Your protagonist has watched enough horror movies to know it's highly unlikely she's going to get out of this alive. But she's also seen enough movies to know her best chance at survival is to bond with her captor and get him to feel empathy for her. Write her inner monologue as she practices various tactics she might use to talk her way out of this situation.

WRITE

Your protagonist is being held captive by a serial killer. Write a scene where the killer gives her a tour of his home and shows her the various trophies he has collected from his other victims. He isn't sure how he's going to want to remember his new victim yet. He needs to get to know her first.

Remember: Your protagonist wants to bond with this man in the hope that she can tap into a shred of compassion that will allow him to let her go. How might she shift this strategy when she discovers that this monster *wants* to get to know her?

OPTIONAL ELEMENTS TO INCLUDE

- A jar of fingernails.
- A piece of jewelry.
- A dog collar.

Horror Twist

Your protagonist clocks several small cameras in the room. She assumes her captor is watching her, but what if she's wrong? What if someone else is watching? What if she's being illegally livestreamed on the dark web into homes of psychopaths across the country? Is there any way she could use these cameras to her own advantage in her efforts to escape?

Eeny, Meeny, Miney, Mo

SCENARIO

Your protagonist wakes up in a dark room. He's dazed, aching, and disoriented. He tries to move but discovers he's chained to a wall. As his eyes adjust to the darkness, he realizes he's not alone. He's in a small space with several other strangers, all sharing the same chains.

BRAINSTORM

When is a choice not a choice? Create a set of rules that this group of strangers must follow for their serial-killer captor to guarantee half of them will survive. It's like a democratic death process: Is it possible for a group of people to fairly decide who lives and who dies?

WRITE

Write a scene where a group of strangers are forced to decide who should die at the hands of their captor. Take them through several options as they each explore their thought processes. The closer they come to a decision, the more chaotic things get.

OPTIONAL ELEMENTS TO INCLUDE

- A desperate plea.
- A sudden, surprising act of violence.
- A hidden weapon.

Horror Twist

Put the killer in the room with them. He doesn't have to hide behind a mask. It's scarier if he appears to be a normal (secretly bloodthirsty) guy.

Stop Trying to Understand Me 

SCENARIO

Your protagonist goes out with a guy she met on a dating app. Maybe he doesn't look quite like his photos, but it's not that unusual for a guy to use old photos on his profile. Sure, it's a red flag, but not an uncommon one. And he's charming enough, so one drink turns into two, two turns into three, and they end up back at his place. You decide how long it takes for her to stumble upon the dead bodies.

BRAINSTORM

The serial killer stalked your protagonist before this date. Not in person—only online. Make a list of everything a stranger could find out about her before they meet. You might even want to do a few searches for yourself to see how exposed you are on the Internet—then use some of those details for your protagonist. How many of her secrets aren't as secret as she might think?

WRITE

Write a scene where your protagonist tries to outsmart her serial-killer captor by bonding with him using some of the information she learned about him before the date went south. What lies did he tell her on their date? What truths did he slip into conversation? Is she able to differentiate between the two? Build to a moment where she hits an emotional nerve.

OPTIONAL ELEMENTS TO INCLUDE

- A kiss—but there's something strange on his breath.
- A severed hand.
- Roaches.

Horror Twist

Some killers keep little trophies; others keep everything. Play around with the idea that this serial killer is deeply attached to his victims, so much so that he refuses to bury them—their corpses are still in his home. What might he do to disguise the putrid odor? Does he keep them in a freezer, or are they hanging out in the living room? How does the sight of these bodies affect your protagonist? Does this vision of her possible future terrify her or spur her into action?

Quick Writes

Set a timer for 15 minutes and do not stop writing until the timer goes off. Do not edit, cross out, or censor yourself. Write down every thought that comes to you.

1. Write a scene where your protagonist wakes up in a makeshift tomb with several other dead bodies. His attacker left him here, thinking he was dead. Can he get out before his captor discovers the truth?
2. Your protagonist is tied up in a serial killer's basement. Write a scene where the killer's mother delivers dinner and your protagonist tries to convince this meek woman to help her escape. She might discover that the woman isn't as meek as she appears.
3. Write a scene where your protagonist escapes her captor's home and retreats to a safe place. But there's something she doesn't know: The serial killer implanted a tracking device under her skin while she was sleeping.
4. Write a scene where your protagonist fights back. She uses one of the serial killer's weapons against him, only to discover that he's stronger than she thought. And now he's angrier than she's ever seen him before.
5. Your protagonist is obsessed with Serial Killer podcasts. Write a scene where he goes on a date with someone he met in an online forum devoted to investigating unsolved crimes. As the night goes on, he begins to suspect his date *is* the serial killer.

GHOSTLY VISIONS

Your protagonist might see them at home, creeping through his house at night. Or maybe he senses them in a crowd and a chill goes down his spine as he realizes he's the only one who sees them. Maybe one of them appears to him at his office and he has to keep working, even though he desperately wants to get as far away from them as possible. You never know when you might have Ghostly Visions, or what they might do to you.

Some people believe young children can see ghosts because they haven't yet formed emotional walls between this world and the next. Kids possess a pure energy that connects them to a higher consciousness or spiritual realm. But as we get older, life beats us down, dulling us to the point that we no longer see the things our logical minds can't explain. The ghosts disappear. We forget what we knew. Which is why it's so scary when the veil is lifted and we see Ghostly Visions as adults—we're used to the wall we've built. We feel safe. We don't want to face the afterlife or think about our own mortality.

When your protagonist begins having Ghostly Visions, consider all the reasons he might have been chosen. Is this a purely random vision, a tragic twist of fate that puts your protagonist in the path of these ghosts? Or have these apparitions appeared here on purpose? As you begin writing, think about what the ghosts want from your protagonist. Because just as your protagonist has desires, so do these spirits. And Ghostly Visions can easily turn ghastly.

I Saw You in My Dreams

SCENARIO

Your protagonist is staying at an unusual location—a hotel that used to be a prison, or an ancient castle, or maybe she's studied some real estate listings and is squatting in a condo that's been staged for potential buyers. Every night, she has a vivid dream about the woman who used to live here. The dreams are so vivid that she has a hard time differentiating them from reality.

BRAINSTORM

Come up with a backstory for the woman who used to live here. She had a tragic end. Imagine you have photographs of seven pivotal moments from her life and describe what you see in each photo. Pick moments that held great significance for her, moments she will never forget, and let the last one you describe be the moment of her death.

WRITE

Write a scene where your protagonist talks to this woman and doesn't yet realize she's a ghost. The dead woman asks your protagonist for a favor. Whatever she asks your protagonist to do, she understands that it will require some sacrifice and will be dangerous. But there isn't anyone else she can ask.

Remember: Your protagonist might not want to do what the woman says, but she also might not have much of a choice. Make sure she understands that the stakes are life or death. If she doesn't want to meet a fate similar to the ghost's, she'd better figure out how to help—and soon.

OPTIONAL ELEMENTS TO INCLUDE

- The ghost enters your protagonist.
- Your protagonist has a vision of her own death.
- Paralysis.

Horror Twist

What if your protagonist's dreams aren't an accident? Is it really a dream if the ghost can enter her subconscious? You might include a moment where your protagonist is sleepwalking but it's the ghost controlling her body—and she wakes up in a nightmare.

Callbacks

Does anyone from the ghost's past know that your protagonist is staying here? If your protagonist tries to help this ghost, it's very likely there are people nearby who do not want her to do the ghost's bidding.

Do Whatever You Have to Do to Me

SCENARIO

Your protagonist starts seeing people inside her home, but only in reflective surfaces. She sees them everywhere from the bathroom mirror to the gleam of her coffee mug. But no one else believes her.

BRAINSTORM

How can the past literally come back to haunt a person? What is your protagonist's ancestry? Is there someone in her family tree who committed terrible misdeeds (e.g., a killer or someone who committed war crimes)? Come up with a backstory for someone your protagonist is linked to but possibly never knew personally. His horrific deeds should be bad enough that his victims would seek revenge any way possible, even if it means coming for one of his descendants.

WRITE

Write a scene where your protagonist is followed by several ghostly apparitions who disappear when she tries to talk to them. Make it so she doesn't know what's real.

OPTIONAL ELEMENTS TO INCLUDE

- A panicked scream.
- Your protagonist falls and hurts herself.
- She is hurled through a window.

Horror Twist

Your protagonist might not believe that her ancestor was a bad person, but these ghosts have proof. Think about how they can make her see and feel the things her ancestor did to them.

Leave Us Alone

SCENARIO

It starts with an unbearable odor coming from under the house. Then, an unexplainable cold spot in the living room. Then they notice one piece of furniture out of place, and no matter how many times they slide it back to the right spot, it keeps moving—and no one in the family did it. The lights keep flickering. And sometimes, late at night, your protagonist hears voices. Taken individually, each sign of spectral visitations doesn't seem like much, but put it all together and your protagonist and her family are getting a little, well, scared out of their minds.

BRAINSTORM

Does this house have a violent history? Has anyone ever died here? Or do the current inhabitants have a connection to the afterlife? Could a ghost be attached to a member of this family? Decide if this is a random haunting or if it's personal. Either way, your protagonist can't live like this much longer.

WRITE

Write a scene where your protagonist tries to ask the ghosts in her house to leave her family alone, but instead of sending them away, she summons them. Her first vision of these ghosts is more horrific than she imagined. What is the last thing she would ever want to see in her home—what is her most vivid and unsettling fear? *That's* what she sees.

OPTIONAL ELEMENTS TO INCLUDE

- Your protagonist senses a spirit touching her, smelling her, tasting her.
- Your protagonist faints.
- Another member of the family levitates.

Horror Twist

Your protagonist has a secret—something she buried deep that no one in her family knows about. But the ghosts know. The ghosts aren't going to let her get away with what she did.

Callbacks

Think about how your protagonist might summon these ghosts. Is there something specific she might say that draws them closer or makes it possible to feel their presence more strongly?

Quick Writes

Set a timer for 15 minutes and do not stop writing until the timer goes off. Do not edit, cross out, or censor yourself. Write down every thought that comes to you.

1. Your protagonist thinks he sees a dead loved one across a crowded room, across the street, or through a window inside a business. Write a scene where he frantically chases the loved one and ends up hurting himself.
2. Your protagonist likes to imagine her dead lover is still with her. Her imagination is so vivid, she sees him often. Write a scene where he finally speaks to her and says she's in danger. The person who murdered him is coming for her too.
3. Write a scene where your protagonist brings flowers to the site of a fatal car crash where someone he knows died. While saying his goodbyes, he hears a voice talking back to him. But then his ghostly loved one disappears just as quickly.
4. Write a scene where your protagonist goes to the morgue to identify a body. When the sheet is lifted, his undead loved one viciously attacks him. Or does he? When your protagonist emerges unscathed, he begins to doubt his own memories.
5. Your protagonist had a near-death experience. Ever since she came back to life, she's felt different somehow. Write a scene where she tells a friend or therapist about her haunting experiences and suddenly senses another presence in the room with them.

EVIL TWIN

They might look exactly alike, but they're moral opposites: the good twin and the bad twin. It might be a fluke of genetics, or maybe their parents preferred one twin over the other and simply didn't bother to nurture the one they didn't like. Now he's screwed up beyond belief—a villain who could have been good if only he'd been shown the love and attention his twin received.

The Evil Twin trope is like the Bad Seed trope on steroids. The fact that this villain has a good, kind, thoughtful sibling makes his perversions that much more pronounced. Whatever havoc he causes will always come back to his sibling in a painful way. He yearns to corrupt his brother, to bring him over to the dark side. These two are forever connected, two halves of the same coin, always at odds. Ultimately, the Evil Twin and his good sibling must face off against each other—the world is too small for both; only one can survive.

When you're writing an Evil Twin story, you might have fun playing with your readers' perceptions. Just as the Evil Twin likes to trick people into believing he's his brother, you might employ the use of an unreliable narrator. Do your readers always know which twin they're following? Consider how satisfying it might be for them to think they're reading about the good twin only to discover they've fallen prey to one of the Evil Twin's nefarious plots.

I've Never Met You Before

SCENARIO

Your protagonist thinks his twin is dead, which puts him in danger because he has no idea his brother is stalking him. The Evil Twin has been slowly inserting himself into your protagonist's life to destroy it. He won't quit until his brother is emotionally and financially destitute or one of them is dead for real. And he doesn't care who else he hurts in the process.

BRAINSTORM

What has the Evil Twin been up to since his alleged death? Come up with a series of crimes he has committed and how he got away with them. Was he always evil, or did something happen that caused his mental break from reality? Back when they were still close, what behavior did your protagonist notice that clued him into the fact that things were *off* with his brother? How does he think his brother died? Has he done anything that makes him feel responsible for his brother's apparent demise?

WRITE

Write a scene where the Evil Twin pretends to be the good twin as he meets up with one of the following: the good twin's significant other, the good twin's boss, the good twin's therapist, or the good twin's best friend. The Evil Twin confesses to a crime the good twin didn't commit. He delivers an Academy Award–worthy performance. Does the person he's meeting with believe it?

Remember: Your protagonist might not talk about his brother very often. As far as he's concerned, that difficult chapter of his life has ended and it's better to leave the past in the past. You decide if the person in this scene knows about the Evil Twin or not.

OPTIONAL ELEMENTS TO INCLUDE

- A stolen kiss.
- A threat.
- Fake tears.

Horror Twist

The Evil Twin has enemies. Think about what he might really want from this encounter. Maybe a drug dealer threatened to kill him if he doesn't pay what he owes, and he knows his brother's confidant has the money he needs. Or maybe he murdered someone and he's looking for someone else to pin the crime on. Whatever his motivation, he is going to ruin more than just his brother's life. Everyone in his brother's circle is in danger.

You Can Trust Me

SCENARIO

Your protagonist has protected her Evil Twin their entire lives. Covering up for her misdeeds, cleaning up her messes, and even taking the fall for some of her missteps. But she can't do it anymore. She wants to get the Evil Twin help.

BRAINSTORM

What exactly makes this Evil Twin *evil*? What's the worst thing she's ever done? Come up with a crime so sinister, so atrocious, so chilling that you shock yourself as you're writing it.

WRITE

Your protagonist wants to take her Evil Twin to a mental institution. Write a scene where she lies to her twin about her intentions, saying she wants to take her away on a vacation. When the Evil Twin discovers it's a lie, she is going to lose her mind.

OPTIONAL ELEMENTS TO INCLUDE

- A call to the police.
- Alcohol.
- A moment of degradation.

Horror Twist

How is evil born? Do both twins have the capacity for evil? What if their parents favored one over the other from an early age, treating one with love and kindness and the other with apathy and anger? Perhaps the twins should team up and teach a lesson to the real villains of their story.

I Dare You to Let Go

SCENARIO

Your protagonist's twin has been experimenting with the occult. He has acquired some sort of power—anything from telekinesis to astral projection to black magic—and he has the worst possible intentions. When your protagonist learns of his sibling's evil extracurricular activities, he knows he must do something. Otherwise, a lot of people are about to die.

BRAINSTORM

Does the twin have any evil allies? Who are the people he trusts most? Who may have helped him acquire his powers? What are they motivated by—greed, pride, wrath, envy, lust, gluttony, sloth? What kind of chaos are they capable of? Consider how much they might enjoy being bad, and how each misdeed fuels their destructive desires.

WRITE

Write a scene where your protagonist reasons with his Evil Twin and tries to get him to abort a plan to cause harm that he's already set in motion; in return, the twin tries to kill your protagonist. This mission is going to be much harder than your protagonist realized.

Remember: Your protagonist doesn't have any powers, but he knows his brother better than anyone else. Can he outsmart his brother by anticipating his worst actions?

OPTIONAL ELEMENTS TO INCLUDE

- A terrifying vision of the future.
- Total darkness.
- A last breath.

Horror Twist

Do you believe in twin telepathy? What if your protagonist can communicate with his twin without words? Or take that further: What if your protagonist can *see* his Evil Twin's intentions? What if he can *feel* his Evil Twin's worst impulses? What if every time the twin does something bad, your protagonist takes on the guilt and regret his Evil Twin doesn't feel? Maybe all this psychological stress awakens something evil in your protagonist?

Quick Writes

Set a timer for 15 minutes and do not stop writing until the timer goes off. Do not edit, cross out, or censor yourself. Write down every thought that comes to you.

1. Your protagonist can't get a break. Her bad luck never seems to run out. Write a scene where she meets an Evil Twin from a parallel dimension. The twin wants to kill your protagonist and take her place.
2. Write a scene where your protagonist sees his twin murder someone. When the twin asks for help covering up his crime, your protagonist finds himself at a crossroads. Whatever he does sends him spiraling down a path of torment.
3. Write a scene where your protagonist performs a spell to bring her dead sibling back to life. It works, but the sibling is different now: evil, supernatural, violent, monstrous.
4. Your protagonist and his twin have spent their entire lives competing. Write a scene where the twin proposes a truce and makes dinner to celebrate. Your protagonist doesn't know that the main ingredient of tonight's "dinner" is his girlfriend or boyfriend.
5. Your protagonist is on a relaxing retreat with his twin and several friends. Write a scene where the twin announces that your protagonist brought them all here to kill them. No one knows which twin to believe. Chaos ensues.

IT RUNS IN THE FAMILY

The family that kills together stays together. It's unlikely you'll find that aphorism imprinted on a welcome mat or embroidered on a throw pillow in anyone's home, but it's the unofficial motto of the violently screwed-up families you'll find in this trope. Murder? Cannibalism? Stalking? Torture? When it comes to these terrors and more, It Runs in the Family.

A family of psychopaths might be formed *by* blood (usually through forbidden—yes, incestuous—couplings within the family) or forged *in* blood (murderous strangers who become a found family together because of their bloodlust). If they're a cannibalistic clan, they're the type of cannibals who like to play with their food.

This may sound strange, but there's a playfulness to these stories. Serial killers are often portrayed as lone wolves, weirdos who can't connect with anyone. But when It Runs in the Family, you've got a group of psychos who are grateful to have found likeminded freaks. And if they're genuinely related to each other, there's a family bond sealed by the most evil inheritance you can imagine.

These characters have their own language only they can understand. They have inside jokes. They even have longstanding feuds, but if someone tried to hurt the family member they hate they would still do anything to protect them. They have their own special kind of love; they just have a horrific way of expressing it.

Brother Knows Best

SCENARIO

Your protagonist hasn't dated in a while. Her last relationship was messy and ended badly. She was dating a slightly older guy, and he went ballistic when she said she wanted to end things. He was violent and out of control. He made her feel so unsafe she was afraid he might kill her. Now she's finally ready to put herself back out there again, and she's met a nice guy her own age.

BRAINSTORM

Write a short profile of your protagonist's ex. What sights, sounds, smells, and tastes remind her of him? What were his likes and dislikes? Did they have any favorite restaurants or TV shows or activities they loved to indulge in together that are forever ruined for her because he tainted them? Are there any verbal tics or phrases that she associates with him?

WRITE

Write a scene where your protagonist goes on a date with her new love interest. You decide how long they've been together—anywhere from a few weeks to a year. The date is going well until he says something that reminds her of her ex. Twist: The ex and her new boyfriend are related. In fact, she didn't meet him by accident. Her new boyfriend sought her out to get revenge for his family member.

Remember: Your protagonist still feels raw from her previous relationship. She was nervous about putting herself out there again. So this feels like more than just a betrayal—it's an emotional bomb, and her reaction will be equally explosive. (That doesn't mean she'll show how upset she is. As soon as she discovers who this man is, she'll understand that she's in danger. It will be a miracle if she gets out of this date alive.)

OPTIONAL ELEMENTS TO INCLUDE

- Several bottles of wine.
- A familiar birthmark.
- Her ex is also here, watching them.

Callbacks

Look at her first date with her ex and her first date with this new guy. Include a few moments in the date with the new guy that echo that first date with her ex—moments she would have seen as warning signs if she hadn't let her guard down.

"You're Kidding Yourself If You Think Evil Skips a Generation"

SCENARIO

Your protagonist grew up among liars, cheaters, killers, con artists, and thieves. He wants nothing to do with them. But lately he's begun feeling a hankering for cruelty. A curiosity he finds disgusting. A yearning to do something wrong. It's as if there's a monster inside him waiting to come out.

BRAINSTORM

Write a brief criminal history for everyone in your protagonist's immediate family. What bad deeds did he witness firsthand, and what stories did he hear? Think about how the actions of his family members affected his psyche.

WRITE

Write a scene where your protagonist seeks out a member of his family he hasn't spoken to in years. He wants advice about how to deal with these unusual cravings. You decide whether this family member welcomes him back into the fold or shuns him.

OPTIONAL ELEMENTS TO INCLUDE

- Eating raw flesh (human or animal).
- Your protagonist talks to himself, and a voice talks back.
- A promise.

Callbacks

When your protagonist looks at this family member, does he recognize himself in them? If he has evil embedded in his DNA, should he just accept his destiny? Is it possible to stave off the wickedness forever?

Your Blood Tastes Like Mine

SCENARIO

Your protagonist and some friends go to a music festival or protest rally—any event with a large group of likeminded strangers where people might be drinking and doing drugs. The atmosphere is jovial. Lots of energy, camaraderie, bonding. One of your protagonist's friends bumps into a group of people he knows: "These are my cousins." The two groups join up. They end up heading to a new location to continue the party.

BRAINSTORM

This new group of "cousins" might be related, or they might not be. But they're *very* close—in a disturbing way. Quickly write a brief description of each cousin; include their main personality traits and behavioral quirks. Who is the leader of the group?

WRITE

Write a scene where the cousins take your protagonist and her friends to a private location and then reveal themselves to be monsters. The party quickly transforms into an all-out violent melee as the cousins attack your protagonist and her friend group. Let the scene be chaotic and confusing. When the initial shock wears off, your protagonist and any remaining survivors are going to have to figure out how to fight back.

Remember: Your protagonist came here because one of her friends vouched for these people. Was he in on it? Was it a trap? Or was he just as surprised by the violence as everyone else? Your protagonist will have to figure out if she can trust this friend or not.

OPTIONAL ELEMENTS TO INCLUDE

- Toxic fumes.
- Your protagonist is bound and gagged.
- A jar full of teeth.

Horror Twist

The cousins are nihilists. They believe life is meaningless. They don't have any sense of morality, and they don't care if they die. All they care about is having fun, and inflicting pain on others feels like fun tonight. There's no reasoning with them.

Quick Writes

Set a timer for 15 minutes and do not stop writing until the timer goes off. Do not edit, cross out, or censor yourself. Write down every thought that comes to you.

1. Write a scene where your protagonist meets his in-laws for the first time and discovers this is a trap. Turns out the family has a pet demon/monster/creature who needs to be fed. It was his fiancée's turn to bring the human sacrifice.
2. Your young protagonist is adopted by a seemingly loving couple. Write a scene where she discovers her new family is a group of witches, werewolves, vampires, or aliens. And they have alarming plans for their new daughter.
3. Write a scene where a feral family (very little language, mutated, strong) invades your protagonist's home, trapping everyone in one room. How will your protagonist and his family get out of here alive?
4. Write a scene where your protagonist moves into a new house and one of the neighbors warns her to stay away from the family in the house across the street: "They do strange things at night."
5. Your teenage protagonist has begun going through puberty, but his body is undergoing changes they didn't talk about in health class. Write a scene where his dad tells him the family secret: "We're monsters."

DEMONIC POSSESSION

A Demonic Possession will send a person into an altered state of consciousness where they lose total control of their body, their mind, and even their spirit. Signs one of your characters is the victim of Demonic Possession:

Violent outbreaks. Sudden blindness, deafness, or muteness. Seizures. Unexplainable bruises. Teeth grinding. Speaking in tongues. Spontaneous cuts. Wild mood swings. Intrusive thoughts. Hostility. Restlessness. Hearing voices. Self-violence. Compulsive behavior. The ability to read thoughts. Knowledge of past misdeeds. Gluttony.

Any character could be possessed by a demon, but your readers are more likely to invest in someone good and decent who suddenly exhibits one or more of the signs listed previously. You want your readers to root for their survival.

One of the fun challenges of writing a Demonic Possession story is creating a protagonist who is a worthy adversary for the Devil himself. Even if your protagonist is flawed and complicated, you want your readers to believe there's at least a *chance* he will be victorious. But there's no guarantee of a happy ending here. Because demons don't die. They just find new hosts. No one is safe.

I'll See You in Hell

SCENARIO

Your protagonist has an awful boss. It doesn't matter what kind of job he has—it could be anything from cashier at a hot dog stand to attorney at a fancy law firm. Your protagonist and his boss have always butted heads. The boss just isn't good with people. But lately, the boss seems worse than usual. He seems like another person, even. That's because the boss from hell has been possessed by a demon from hell. And now your protagonist's life is going to hell too.

BRAINSTORM

Is your protagonist good at conflict resolution? Freewrite about how he typically handles interpersonal conflicts at work. Can these skills come into play when he's fighting a literal monster?

WRITE

Write a scene where your protagonist and a few other coworkers begin to suspect their boss is possessed. Possible signs: The office is silent, but he orders everyone to stop talking; he explodes in rage, spouting Latin and curse words, without any provocation; he vomits a putrid concoction of blood and mucus all over your protagonist. Something is clearly wrong.

Remember: Your protagonist is used to the boss being a jerk, so it might take a while to realize there's more to it than that. You might let your readers in on the truth first so you can build tension around the question of when your protagonist will figure out he's in danger.

OPTIONAL ELEMENTS TO INCLUDE

- Snakes.
- A supply closet filled with dead bodies.
- Fire.

Horror Twist

Is demonic possession contagious? If someone you know gets possessed by a demon, does that mean you're more likely to get possessed too? Think about how you might raise the stakes of your story by having more than one character get possessed. What would your protagonist do if everyone at the office tried to lure him into evil? Could he fight them all off?

Callbacks

Go back to the moment when your protagonist interviewed for this job. Did his boss ask, "Where do you see yourself in five years?" Compare his answer to the way his life looks now. How do his struggles with his possessed boss thematically speak to the fact that he isn't doing what he wants to be doing with his life?

I'm Broken

SCENARIO

Your protagonist is estranged from his adult daughter. Before she went no-contact, they had a fight where your protagonist said things he wishes he could take back. He was so afraid of losing her that he lashed out in anger. He hasn't heard from her since, and he's haunted by his words. So, when he gets a call from one of her friends saying that she needs him, he thanks God for a second chance. Unfortunately, this is not the second chance he was expecting.

BRAINSTORM

How long have your protagonist and his daughter been apart? How many big moments in her life has he missed? What was she hoping to do with her life, and how has she failed to fulfill her dreams? Come up with at least ten bad choices she's made since she went no-contact. Imagine how things might have gone differently for her if she'd had better parental guidance.

WRITE

Write a scene where your protagonist shows up for a meeting with his daughter. He's prepared to apologize and grovel, if that's what it takes. He will do whatever he needs to do to get her back into his good graces. But then her friend gives him the bad news: She has been possessed by the Devil. And they need your protagonist's help to get the evil out.

Remember: Your protagonist has lost his daughter once; he has no intention of losing her again. Would he go so far as to sacrifice his own life to save hers?

OPTIONAL ELEMENTS TO INCLUDE

- Your protagonist comes prepared with a written speech.
- His daughter's skin is covered in burns and boils.
- A sweltering heat.

Horror Twist

Think about how this possession manifests itself physically. Does she grow horns and fangs? A tail? Is her skin hot to the touch? Can she breathe fire? Do wings burst out of her shoulder blades?

Callbacks

What does your protagonist most regret saying during their big relationship-ending fight? Have her reference his hurtful words during this scene where they reunite. But it isn't his daughter speaking; it's the demon inside her—a demon who knows all their baggage.

"Let Go of Him—He Doesn't Belong to You"

SCENARIO

Your protagonist is a priest who has been performing exorcisms for decades. He's been asked to meet with a man to determine if he's been possessed. This man has already been through a series of psychiatric and medical evaluations. But your protagonist is wary—most of these calls turn out to be a waste of time.

BRAINSTORM

Write a brief history of your protagonist's demonic interactions. How many exorcisms has he performed? How many scars (physical and emotional) has he acquired from them?

WRITE

Write a scene where your protagonist meets this potentially possessed man for the first time. He is skeptical as he begins to go through his routine interview questions. But as they talk, the man says something that makes your protagonist realize the man is actually possessed by a demon your protagonist has met before. A demon who almost killed him.

OPTIONAL ELEMENTS TO INCLUDE

- Demonic vexation (a physical attack).
- Demonic obsession (a mental attack).
- Holy water.

Callbacks

Write the scene where your protagonist and this demon first met. This was an almost deadly exorcism. How might the details of this earlier exorcism inform his actions now? What did he learn from his last run-in with this evil presence?

Quick Writes

Set a timer for 15 minutes and do not stop writing until the timer goes off. Do not edit, cross out, or censor yourself. Write down every thought that comes to you.

1. Your protagonist's mother/father/sibling has been possessed by a violent demon. Write a scene where your protagonist tries to calm his loved one down (while waiting for the priest to show up) but the loved one bites him. Hard.
2. Write a scene where your protagonist meets with a medium to deliver a message to a recently deceased loved one. Instead of reaching her loved one, your protagonist encounters a demon who takes over her body, determined to take care of some unfinished business.
3. Write a scene where a demon inhabits your protagonist's body and breaks into a tomb or catacomb with the intention of opening a portal to hell. The dead will rise tonight!
4. A group of strangers accept a challenge to stay overnight in a haunted house in the hope of winning prize money. Write a scene where one of the competitors is possessed by an angry spirit and the rest of the group scrambles to save them.
5. Write a comedic horror scene where your protagonist attends his weekly therapy session, but the therapist has no idea that he's currently possessed by a narcissistic ghost. The ghost has major problems he needs to work through.

GOING VIRAL

You've heard people say, "Love is in the air." Well, so is evil. Sometimes literally. It can appear in the form of a virus. And the scariest thing about a virus is that no one can see it coming.

One day your protagonist is going about her daily routine, pursuing the dream she no longer has much hope of reaching, trying to mend things with the ex she still has feelings for, working on improving the strained relationship she has with her teenage kid, and just generally getting her life together, and then *wham*. Her neighbor gets sick. Then one of her kid's teachers becomes ill, and they start hearing more and more stories about some strange sickness ravaging other cities. Then she gets a call from her ex, telling her not to come over—he's afraid of passing this strange sickness on to her.

It isn't a normal sickness. This is a virus that might infect your characters with madness or anger. A virus that might make your characters suicidal or murderous. A virus that could even cause them to mutate. Your protagonist might visit her ex and see his flesh rotting off, or maybe he's transforming into a flesh-eating reptilian creature, or maybe he's been poisoned with so much anger he wants to rip your protagonist's head off—and suddenly he's strong enough to do it.

In the end, your protagonist will go on the run to protect her loved ones and avoid contamination. But ultimately there's no hiding from evil when it's Going Viral.

It's Inside Me

SCENARIO

Your protagonist was exposed to the virus. He goes to the only person he trusts and asks them to lock him up. He instructs his friend not to let him out under any circumstances until they know for certain that he hasn't been infected, or until they find a cure. No matter what he says, no matter how much he begs, *do not let him out.*

BRAINSTORM

How far back do these friends go? What trials have they been through? How much adversity have they faced by each other's sides? Think about how hard it might be for the friend to see your protagonist in pain. But they deeply respect each other, and the friend will not break. (Or will he? You decide.) Explore what the friend might risk by keeping your protagonist locked up, and what he might lose if your protagonist is contagious and goes free.

WRITE

Write a scene where your protagonist asks his friend to let him out. The friend refuses. Your protagonist demands to be let out. The friend refuses again, fearing the worst. Your protagonist is adamant that he feels fine; he's not sick. They fight. Make it the worst fight of their lives.

Remember: Your protagonist and his friend go way back, so your protagonist knows how to manipulate his friend and really get under his skin. If he's been infected by the virus, he might play dirty as he attempts to break free. How cruel can he get with his friend?

OPTIONAL ELEMENTS TO INCLUDE

- Sweat, mucus, and tears.
- Banging on glass.
- The key to the cage is lost.

Horror Twist

Try flipping the entire scenario around. What if your protagonist hasn't caught the virus, but the friend standing guard outside his cage *is* infected? Instead of begging for freedom, your protagonist desperately wants to stay inside the cage. But that means he will have to watch his friend go crazy or maybe even die. He is trapped by the cruelty of this viral outbreak.

"I'm Sorry, but I Can't Leave Without Him"

SCENARIO

Your protagonist must evacuate his apartment building. A virus is raging through the city, and their only hope of survival is to flee. But some of his neighbors don't want to go.

BRAINSTORM

Think about how hard it would be to leave everything you've ever known. Some horrors leave deep emotional scars. Sometimes it's easier to give up. Do some freewriting about everything this epidemic will take from your protagonist. How will he navigate so much loss?

WRITE

Write a scene where your protagonist tries to convince an elderly neighbor to leave with them. This is someone he's close to, who has been like a surrogate grandparent to him, but she has decided to stay. Her husband or child is infected, and she will not abandon them. Your protagonist doesn't want to accept this. If she stays, she dies too. Can he convince her?

OPTIONAL ELEMENTS TO INCLUDE

- Sirens in the distance.
- A dead body in the hallway.
- Dead birds falling from the sky.

Horror Twist

What if the virus has already reached the building? Your protagonist can hear the infected banging at the doors outside as he tries to reason with his neighbor.

No!

SCENARIO

Your protagonist is on the run with a loved one. It might be her husband, or one of her parents, or her child. They've fallen in with a group of strangers who are looking for a safe place to find shelter. Your protagonist's loved one is infected, but your protagonist is doing everything she can to hide that fact from the others.

BRAINSTORM

Think about different ways this virus might be transmitted. Is it airborne? Does it require a transfer of fluids? Skin-to-skin contact? If an infected person bites someone, does that seal the victim's fate? Come up with a few other less traditional possibilities. What if the virus could be transmitted through a glance? Or what if it had to be consumed? Could it be passed on through an emotion?

WRITE

Write a scene where someone else in the group discovers your protagonist's secret. Tempers quickly flare when they realize your protagonist has put everyone in danger by hiding her loved one's sickness. A fight ensues. The group makes the only decision they can: They must kill the loved one.

Remember: Your protagonist isn't acting rationally. If this weren't her loved one, she would probably want them dead too. But since it *is* her loved one, she is going to hate the people responsible for their death. From this moment on, she will see them as enemies. And she will want justice.

OPTIONAL ELEMENTS TO INCLUDE

- A switchblade.
- People have to hold your protagonist back.
- The loved one's body is cremated.

Callbacks

Your protagonist will never forget the moment when she is forced to watch her loved one die. Keep this event alive for her throughout the rest of your story, and think about how this moment changes and hardens her.

Quick Writes

Set a timer for 15 minutes and do not stop writing until the timer goes off. Do not edit, cross out, or censor yourself. Write down every thought that comes to you.

1. Your protagonist is taking care of an ailing family member who sees movement under her skin, like insects slithering around. Write a scene where she begs your protagonist to cut her sickness out of her flesh—and if your protagonist won't help, she'll do it herself.
2. A group of refugees are hiding in an abandoned home goods store. Write a scene where one of the characters inhales some fumes, then undergoes a transformation. He raids the aisles for anything he can use as a weapon against the others in his group.
3. Your protagonist is in a huge crowd at a sports arena, a concert venue, or a movie theater. Something foul is in the air. She's enjoying herself until she notices people getting agitated around her. The crowd has been infected with rage, and they want blood.
4. Write a scene where your protagonist discovers his daughter has a virus that turns people into vicious cannibals. There's no cure. The only safe and sane thing to do is to end her misery. But can he do it?
5. A plague has ravaged the city. Your protagonist is hiding in a bunker with her family and a few friends. They're safe here. They hear someone outside, begging to come in. Write a scene where they debate what to do.

A TOWN'S SINISTER SECRET

There's an unwritten law of the universe that says all secrets must come out, but there's at least one exception: When a whole town is guarding the same Sinister Secret, they will do everything they can to keep it hidden. In a town where evil lives just below the surface, these secrets can insidiously create havoc and misery. Anyone who comes close to learning the truth will put themself at risk.

Enter your protagonist. He's new in town and naively thinks he will not feel like an outsider for long. But he quickly discovers he doesn't fit in at all. Your protagonist is seen as a threat by many townspeople, so they keep him at a distance. He can't be allowed to know the truth about what's going on here.

Ironically, the fact that people don't let your protagonist in is what makes him suspicious. If they were a little more welcoming, maybe he wouldn't go digging for answers.

What's he going to find? There are so many creepy and dangerous options: an underground drug ring, a Satanic cult, a coven of witches and warlocks. Or maybe there's an elite club of women who have toppled the patriarchy and turned their husbands into subservient robots. Or everyone in the town is being experimented on by aliens who have replaced them with replicants. The possibilities are endless.

Your protagonist is a problem. He is a threat to this town's existence. They're going to have to deal with him before he learns something he shouldn't.

What Does Your Tattoo Mean?

SCENARIO

Your protagonist moves to a quaint small town. She has a new job, she's making friends, and she even meets a handsome guy who asks her out. But during dinner, when she asks him about the strange tattoo on his arm—the same tattoo she noticed on one of her coworkers earlier—something switches for this guy. His attitude shifts. He's not interested in her anymore. What did she say?

BRAINSTORM

Do some research into secret societies and the symbols they use to identify members. Come up with the perfect tattoo for members of the secret society you are creating.

WRITE

Write a scene where your protagonist discreetly follows her date, spying on him and trying to learn why he was acting so strangely. She suspects he might have a wife, but instead she discovers something much more upsetting: some sort of underground gathering of hundreds of men. What are they hiding?

OPTIONAL ELEMENTS TO INCLUDE

- A man removes the skin from his face.
- A man eats a live rat.
- The group performs a human sacrifice.

Callbacks

Did your protagonist ask her coworker about his tattoo? What can she learn from her coworker's and her date's strange reactions?

Who Were You Talking To?

SCENARIO

Your protagonist is a novelist, a screenwriter, or another type of artist, and he's on a creative retreat in a small town. The person who runs the inn or bed-and-breakfast where he's staying gives him strict instruction not to go outside after dark, with a vague warning about wildlife. But your protagonist suspects something else is going on, so he sneaks out one night.

BRAINSTORM

Your protagonist doesn't like to follow rules. It's part of his identity as a creative type, which means that when he senses a story somewhere, he will seek it out. Come up with a few small moments early in your story that could make people in town grow suspicious of him. How could he earn the reputation of "nosy neighbor"?

WRITE

Your protagonist tries to leave in the middle of the night and discovers his bedroom door is locked from the outside. These people really don't want him to leave! Write a scene where he calls a friend back home and theorizes what might be going on in this strange town; during this call, he is interrupted by the innkeeper, who wants to know what he knows.

Remember: The more paranoia these townspeople exhibit, the more your protagonist will look for answers. Make sure their secret is a big one: Perhaps they perform pagan rituals every night to ward off evil spirits, or maybe nighttime is when the vampires come out to play (and the locals are trying to protect your protagonist).

OPTIONAL ELEMENTS TO INCLUDE

- Your protagonist is being recorded.
- An unexpected storm.
- The innkeeper lies about his family history.

Horror Twist

What if your protagonist is an unknowing participant in a scientific experiment, and everyone in town is in on it? They might be studying the biology of fear and how it impacts a human's day-to-day behavior. In which case, things are only going to get worse for him from here on out.

“I Saw Them Heading Into the Woods”

SCENARIO

Your married protagonists just moved to a remote village where they immediately get creeped out by the locals. Either everyone's *too* nice, or they're extremely standoffish, or maybe they have a distant look in their eyes that feels . . . inhuman.

BRAINSTORM

This couple moved here hoping it would shake up their lives. They're having trust issues. Come up with three problems that plague their marriage—things they need to work on if they want this relationship to last.

WRITE

It's a Sunday afternoon. Your protagonists head out for brunch at a local diner or coffee shop, and they're surprised to discover no one is around. The town square is literally empty. Write a scene where they work together to investigate.

Remember: They may not be able to see eye to eye these days, but they agree there's something extremely weird going on in this town. Maybe the creepy activities of their neighbors will help them mend their marriage?

OPTIONAL ELEMENTS TO INCLUDE

- An elderly woman shares a story from the town's past.
- Chanting.
- A cryptic note.

Horror Twist

Whatever this town is hiding, make it something your protagonists will wish they'd never learned about. Unspeakable violence. Wild perversions. Murder and mayhem.

Quick Writes

Set a timer for 15 minutes and do not stop writing until the timer goes off. Do not edit, cross out, or censor yourself. Write down every thought that comes to you.

1. Your protagonist's employer transfers her to a satellite office in a small town. Write a scene where she has a sudden realization: Since she moved, she's never heard any birds, seen anyone walking a dog, or noticed a stray cat. There are *no* animals anywhere.
2. Your protagonist moved to a small town to look for his missing sister. Write a scene where he searches the town and keeps meeting women who look almost exactly like her. Almost as if they're clones.
3. Your protagonist's friend goes missing. When she starts investigating, she discovers a series of hushed-up disappearances. Write a scene where she confronts a member of the city government, who tells her to stop digging or else. What the heck's going on?
4. When your protagonist gets home from his first service at a new church, he feels confused and disoriented. Almost as if he's been drugged. Write a scene where he attends another service and decides not to take communion. This time he feels fine. Weird, right?
5. Your protagonist recently joined his kids' school's parent-teacher association. Write a scene where he stumbles into the wrong breakout group and discovers two teachers eating one of the school's "bad" kids. What. The. Hell?

BAD SEED

It's a mother's worst nightmare. The deep bond she was certain she would feel for the rest of her life suddenly transforms when her perfect child becomes something else entirely—a creature who could take his mother's life and never look back.

Ideally, your readers won't see the Bad Seed trope coming until a string of unsolved murders raises suspicion in the one place they thought was safe: the beautiful home where a frightened mother has taken every possible precaution to protect her child from whatever is out there.

The problem is, whenever the mother isn't looking, the child does something alarming. Maybe he wipes his mouth with the back of his hand and what his mother thought was strawberry jam turns out to be blood. Or perhaps the little boy places objects in his mother's path that result in falls, broken bones, and emergency room visits. And why does that kitchen knife keep ending up in his toy chest?

A mother knows when something is not right with her child. But it takes time to face the terrible truth that a Bad Seed has come from your womb and put down roots in what you thought would be a safe and happy home. Take your readers on a harrowing journey as the mother slowly realizes her child is evil incarnate. Remember, a Bad Seed is never a product of bad parenting. They're born this way, and once a parent realizes this, the real battle begins. Because a Bad Seed is capable of anything.

It Was Just an Accident

SCENARIO

"It was just an accident." That's what your protagonist's Bad Seed told the police after his friend died under mysterious circumstances. He said it repeatedly: "It was just an accident." He stuck to his story and appeared to be distraught. But your protagonist doesn't believe a word that comes out of her son's mouth. She knows him too well.

BRAINSTORM

Does your protagonist recognize any of herself in her son? When she was younger, did she have a viciousness within her that she's pushed away? Come up with three traits within the Bad Seed that your protagonist identifies with. Imagine a moment from their past when she tried to connect with him but came up short.

WRITE

Write a scene (or series of scenes) where your protagonist sets out to uncover the truth about what happened to her son's friend. But the closer she gets to the truth, the more danger she's in.

OPTIONAL ELEMENTS TO INCLUDE

- Muddy sneakers.
- A lock of hair.
- A dare.

Horror Twist

Proving a crime happened is difficult when you don't have any tangible evidence. What if the friend's body is missing as well? How might the Bad Seed have disposed of his friend's remains?

I'll Tell Daddy

SCENARIO

Your protagonist is tired of the gaslighting. When other people are around, her kid's an angel; but when it's just the two of them, he's cruel and sadistic. Your protagonist dreads spending time with him. She feels like she's living in a nightmare, and she's desperate to get others to see what she knows her child is capable of.

BRAINSTORM

Your protagonist always wanted to be a mom. The reality isn't what she expected. Make a list of regrets and disappointments she's had to face since she became a mother, and think about how difficult it is for her to come to terms with her current reality. Make a list of ten moments she shared with her child that helped her realize he's a psychopath. Think of more than just petty grievances. These are life-shattering mental and emotional recalibrations she's had to make.

WRITE

Write a scene where your protagonist is getting ready to tell someone the truth about her child—anyone from a friend to the police. Her child stops her by revealing he knows a secret of hers—something big that she wouldn't want anyone to find out. Is there any way she can let people know the truth about her child without exposing her own secret?

Remember: Your protagonist is feeling so desperate; there will come a point where she won't care about anything other than getting away from this monster—her own secrets be damned.

OPTIONAL ELEMENTS TO INCLUDE

- Scuffed knuckles.
- A piercing scream.
- A misunderstanding.

Horror Twist

The Bad Seed makes your protagonist feel so alone. Is that his evil superpower? What if he turned everyone against her, from her own parents to her friends to her spouse? Is it possible to drive someone mad by removing all their sources of companionship and comfort?

Callbacks

Think about the private language your protagonist and her spouse share. Is there any way she could convey her feelings about their child to her spouse without the demon spawn knowing?

Next Time, I Won't Be So Nice 

SCENARIO

Your Bad Seed character will do anything to get what she wants. She has a terrible temper and a malicious spirit. She has beaten and abused her parents (literally, metaphorically, or both) to the point of defeat. She can get away with whatever she wants—at least, that's what she thinks. But maybe there's still a little bit of fight left in her parents.

BRAINSTORM

There have been countless stories about predators preying on the young and weak, but what if you inverted this dynamic? What does it look like for a child to prey on adults? How does the Bad Seed gain control over people? What are her greatest strengths and weaknesses? And how does the Bad Seed's age affect the kinds of power games she plays? Think about how her reign of terror evolves as she grows older, stronger, smarter, meaner, and more defiant.

WRITE

Write a scene where the Bad Seed punishes her parents for a slight misdeed. The "sin" her parents committed is nothing compared to her response. The punishment can be either physical or emotional/mental, but whatever the Bad Seed does to them will make marks—deep wounds her parents will feel for years.

Remember: The Bad Seed character is your antagonist. Show your readers how deeply she deserves that designation. "Evil" doesn't even begin to describe her actions. Make your readers ache for her parents and root for them to break free of the Bad Seed's control.

OPTIONAL ELEMENTS TO INCLUDE

- A moment of joy or hope that is quickly quashed.
- A sudden shove.
- A hidden cell phone.

Horror Twist

Think about the Bad Seed character in animalistic terms, as if she has a wild beast inside her. How might that change the way she speaks, moves, and behaves? Think about what might trigger her wildest impulses. When does the animal come out?

Quick Writes

Set a timer for 15 minutes and do not stop writing until the timer goes off. Do not edit, cross out, or censor yourself. Write down every thought that comes to you.

1. Write a scene where your protagonist witnesses your Bad Seed character pushing an older authority figure off a building or cliff. The child feigns innocence, but your protagonist knows what he saw.
2. Write a scene where your protagonist is trapped in a small, confined space by your Bad Seed character. He tries to negotiate with the Bad Seed, but this kid wants him dead. Your protagonist will have to be clever if he wants to get out of here alive.
3. Write a scene where your protagonist tries to convince her husband that their child is a Bad Seed. She has no idea that her evil offspring is eavesdropping on their conversation.
4. Write a scene where your protagonist is arrested for a crime his child committed, but when he tries to explain himself, no one believes him. They think he's more than just a terrible parent: They think *he's* the psychopath.
5. Write a scene where your protagonist is forced to choose between two of her children—perhaps there's room for only one on a lifeboat, or maybe a fascist government is separating kids from their families as a form of population control. Whatever the reason, she realizes too late: She gave up the wrong kid.

VENGEANCE IS MINE

English poet George Herbert once said, "Living well is the best revenge." But in a horror story, death is often the thing that makes revenge so sweet. Most readers of this genre don't shrink from graphic violence, so make your tale of vengeance as ghastly as possible.

There are other ways to go, however, that are less bloody and equally compelling. Think *Fatal Attraction*. Give your protagonist a good reason to terrorize someone who did her wrong and launch all-out psychological warfare. (Sorry, the *Fatal Attraction* bunny-boiling scene is taken, but there are many other wicked ways to get even with an ex for pulling the plug on the relationship.)

You might also consider a supernatural quest for revenge—perhaps a ghost haunts someone they have good reason to hate, or a Dracula figure goes after the blood of people who are victimizing the vulnerable for financial gain.

The best revenge tales involve intricate plots that draw readers into their protagonist's process of planning and preparing to destroy the person who did them wrong. Throw plenty of obstacles in the way to increase the suspense, and make your protagonist so obsessed with revenge that the lines between protagonist and antagonist begin to blur. Who is the true villain of a story when the "good" character is desperate to proclaim, "Vengeance Is Mine"?

I Think about You Every Day

SCENARIO

Something terrible happened to your protagonist. She's carried this trauma for years. It bubbles up when she least expects it. She tells herself the therapy is working. But the fact that the architect of her trauma is still out there somewhere makes her blood boil. Then one day he walks into her place of employment. He doesn't recognize her, but he'll remember soon enough.

BRAINSTORM

Your protagonist has fantasized about this moment. She's visualized all the different ways it could go. Write ten different interactions between her and this monster from her past. Write an angry version, a calm-and-collected version, a violent version, a version where he remembers her, a version where he pretends he doesn't remember her, a version where he has no idea who she is, a version where she doesn't recognize him at first and the realization feels like a punch to the gut. Explore all the psychic scars created by unspeakable trauma.

WRITE

Write a scene where your protagonist abducts this man. Nothing will keep her from getting her revenge. She feels like a shattered human, and if she lets him get away now, there won't be any way for her to put the pieces back together again. She is determined to break him.

Remember: Think about how much planning this takes. Your protagonist isn't an action movie star. As badass as she might think she is, she's just a regular person. She's *definitely* not the type of person who *abducts* people. Think about all the ways this could go wrong.

OPTIONAL ELEMENTS TO INCLUDE

- A wound that won't stop bleeding.
- A sword.
- An unexpected revelation.

Horror Twist

What if your protagonist's anger is too big to contain? What if her emotions are so visceral that they come to life? Perhaps she coughs up a phlegmy hairball that has claws and teeth, her anger manifested in physical form. How might she use this angry creature as a catalyst of revenge?

Trust Me—You're Dead

SCENARIO

Your protagonist is dead. But that won't stop him from getting revenge against his killer. He won't rest until his assailant is in hell.

BRAINSTORM

How many ways might a person come back from the dead? Your protagonist could come back as a ghost or spirit; he might possess someone, taking over their body against their will; or he could even return via a miraculous act of reincarnation, taking over a dying body just as the previous occupant's spirit lets go. Think of your protagonist's return as an act of willpower. He wanted this so badly that he makes it happen against all odds.

WRITE

Write a series of scenes where your protagonist discreetly taunts his killer. Moments where the killer senses his presence but never sees him. Can he drive his killer crazy?

OPTIONAL ELEMENTS TO INCLUDE

- A dreamlike vision that turns nightmarish.
- Your protagonist bites his assailant.
- Fire.

Horror Twist

Haunting a person can take an emotional and physical toll. Think about how the act of becoming a ghost, possessing another person's body, or even taking a body over via reincarnation might affect your protagonist's mind. How would it complicate your story if his anger drove him mad?

"I'll Make You Feel It on the Inside"

SCENARIO

The antihero at the center of your story thought his life would be different. He's miserable and blames someone from his past. Maybe a bully from school, his parents, or an ex. He is obsessed with this person from his past, and he's determined to ruin their life and make them pay for causing him so much pain. (You decide if his feelings are justified or not; either way, he won't accept responsibility for how much his life sucks.)

BRAINSTORM

Catalogue your protagonist's obsession. He knows everything about this person from his past. Their Internet searches. What they eat every day. What they watch on TV. What apps they use most. Their daily routine. Who they're sleeping with. Their financial situation. Everything. What are the most unusual things your protagonist might have learned about this person?

WRITE

Write a scene where your protagonist finally confronts this person from his past. Make it messy and awkward. By the end of their encounter, your protagonist is even more convinced that this person is responsible for his bad luck and that the only way he'll ever find happiness is by shattering this other person's life. Set that journey in motion.

Remember: The deeper your protagonist sinks into his obsession, the more violent his actions will get. At the beginning of your story, you don't want to have him too far gone just yet. Make sure you have plenty of runway for him to get deeper and deeper into his mania.

OPTIONAL ELEMENTS TO INCLUDE

- Your protagonist has photos of this person sleeping.
- Your protagonist goes through this person's trash.
- Your protagonist confronts one of this person's family members.

Callbacks

Think about how your protagonist's memories might differ from how this person from his past remembers things. From the other character's point of view, has your protagonist always been the aggressor?

Quick Writes

Set a timer for 15 minutes and do not stop writing until the timer goes off. Do not edit, cross out, or censor yourself. Write down every thought that comes to you.

1. Your protagonist keeps tabs on an ex who wronged her. Write a scene where she meets another woman he wronged and convinces her to join her revenge plot.
2. Your protagonist died at the hands of a killer. Write a scene where he possesses the body of someone in the killer's life—with the sole purpose of stealing the killer's soul.
3. Write a scene where your protagonist attempts to poison her enemy but the wrong person ingests the contaminated food/drink. Now her enemy knows someone is after him . . .
4. Your protagonist has been wrongfully imprisoned. He has endured torture and humiliation by a sadistic guard. Write a scene where he turns the tables and imprisons the guard. What will be his first act of revenge? His second? His third?
5. Your protagonist has the worst boss in the world. She's been the victim of bullying, sabotage, gaslighting, and various forms of degradation. Write a scene where she lays out a plan for revenge with several of her coworkers. They decide to go for it.

THE FINAL GIRL

The Final Girl is the ultimate survivor. She's been to hell and back. She has been chased, beaten, mauled, and maimed. She's seen the death of one friend after another, many of them dying right in front of her, their lives brutally taken.

When your readers first meet her, she might not seem like the type of person who's going to survive a horror story—but by the time she earns the adjective "final," she has grown into the role. She has no choice but to be brave now. She has nothing left to lose.

If you're writing a first-person narrative, the Final Girl will be the one telling the story. But that doesn't mean your readers can trust everything she says. She's been through so much trauma that she's bound to be an unreliable narrator. There might be fragments of the story she gets wrong. She might change some of the facts to protect the memories of those she lost. She might even try to make herself look more virtuous and heroic than she really is.

That's no big deal, because no one's alive to correct her. This story is hers to tell. After all she's been through, she can be forgiven for stretching the truth. Right?

Try Me

SCENARIO

Your protagonist was brutally attacked by your antagonist and left for dead, but she was playing possum. It was harrowing and scary for her *not* to run, yet she knew she wasn't fast enough—she knew the attacker would eventually catch up to her. Faking it was the only way she could possibly escape his clutches. It was her only hope.

BRAINSTORM

When you write your protagonist's "death" scene, you might want to fake out your readers as well. Let them think she's dead so they'll be just as surprised as the antagonist to learn the truth. Think about everything she does during the period of your story where she's missing from the narrative. How is she able to hide successfully, and how does she plan to get rid of the antagonist when she returns?

WRITE

Write a scene where your protagonist surprises the antagonist and catches him off guard. She may have even set a trap for him. And now that they're face-to-face again, she is going to take him down just like he took down all her friends, cut by cut by cut. She's going to make him regret every brutal act of violence he ever committed.

Remember: Your protagonist has a lot of tricks up her sleeve. She understands that the antagonist will be difficult to kill, so she's going to come into this battle with contingency plans.

OPTIONAL ELEMENTS TO INCLUDE

- A venomous snake.
- Your protagonist gives the antagonist a choice between two forms of punishment.
- A beheading.

Horror Twist

This entire ordeal has turned your protagonist into an angry, vengeful person. She doesn't recognize herself in the mirror. Her heart is full of hate. Even if she kills the killer, it won't bring her friends back. Think about the life she's going to lead after this. Will she ever find peace and happiness again, or will she always be looking over her shoulder? In the end, maybe this loss of humanity is the true horror story.

Get Rid of Me—I Dare You 

SCENARIO

Your protagonist has taken on an alternate identity. She's living a new life in a new town where no one knows her past. But then the killer finds her.

BRAINSTORM

How much effort did your protagonist put into her new persona? Did she change her hair, style, or mannerisms? Has she tried pursuing new interests and hobbies? Come up with at least ten substantial changes she's made.

WRITE

Write a scene where your protagonist is at her new place of employment and the killer shows up posing as a client or customer. Would he kill her in front of her coworkers?

Remember: Your protagonist is in disguise. Does the killer recognize her, or is she able to evade detection long enough to leave the premises?

OPTIONAL ELEMENTS TO INCLUDE

- Your protagonist triggers the fire alarm.
- A new coworker is killed.
- The killer is also in disguise.

Horror Twist

Instead of making this a slow-burn attack, you might jump right to the scary stuff. What if the killer enters your protagonist's workplace and immediately attacks her, before she knows he's there? Let the killer sneak up on her so your readers can feel the terror before she turns around.

"I've Been Dreaming of This Moment"

SCENARIO

Your protagonist has spent weeks, months, maybe even years in hiding. A psycho killer murdered all her loved ones, so she got as far away as she could. Ever since she disappeared, she's been prepping for the ultimate revenge through a regimen of physical, mental, and weapons training. When she encounters that psycho again, she will be ready.

BRAINSTORM

Map out your protagonist's daily routine. How much does she exercise? What does she eat? What weapon is she most adept with? Imagine she is preparing for the Olympics of death, and figure out all her strengths and weaknesses.

WRITE

Write a scene where your protagonist either turns the tables and stalks the killer who's been after her this whole time, or sets herself up as bait to lure him to her. And this time she's prepared for him. She's stronger than ever, and angrier too. That anger is like fuel. She's ready to brutalize this killer just like he brutalized her friends. She's ready to put on a show.

Remember: Your protagonist is only human. So, as prepared as she may be, she might not get out of this completely unscathed. But whatever battle wounds she receives, she will wear them like badges of honor.

OPTIONAL ELEMENTS TO INCLUDE

- A hatchet.
- A machete.
- A flamethrower.

Horror Twist

Think about this killer's powers. What if he's a shape-shifter and chooses to appear in the form of one of her dead friends? Would that throw her off her game enough for him to get the upper hand? He's strong enough to destroy her physically, but can he also get into her head to destroy her psychologically?

Quick Writes

Set a timer for 15 minutes and do not stop writing until the timer goes off. Do not edit, cross out, or censor yourself. Write down every thought that comes to you.

1. Write a scene where a killer traps your Final Girl in a small, confined space. Can she get out of here before she runs out of air?
2. Write a scene where your antagonist brutally maims your Final Girl, but the more he hurts her the stronger she gets. She unleashes all her fury on him and gets the upper hand. If she ends up dead in the end, is it still considered a win if he died first?
3. Your Final Girl killed the killer, but there's something nagging at her. Write a scene where she confronts another character and accuses him of being the killer's accomplice. When he attacks her, she knows his answer.
4. Write a scene where your Final Girl meets another Final Girl for coffee. They compare notes, bonding over their mutual stories of survival. But can there ever really be two Final Girls? As they talk, a stranger watches them from the shadows.
5. It's been ages since your Final Girl vanquished the demonic spirit that killed her friends. Write a scene where she learns of a new murder that reminds her of what she went through all those years ago. Could her tormentor be back?

ONE LAST SCARE

You're almost at the end of your story. The characters who've survived are dusting themselves off and putting the pieces of their lives back together. They've killed the monster, they've sent the demon back to hell, they've rid their home of ghosts, and so on. On the surface, everything's resolved. They have no idea that One Last Scare still awaits them. But you've plotted a final turn of the screw for them to face, a twist or reveal that will make your readers gasp.

One Last Scare is the horror writer's equivalent of a serial killer twisting the knife in his victim's heart one final time to make sure they're good and dead. This is the moment that will make your readers slam their book shut as they scream out in terror—or make them shudder as they put the book down because they're so unsettled and creeped out by that last image. Leave them with the uneasy feeling that they might not ever be able to shake this dread.

This final story beat might be a moment of true finality—perhaps the death of your protagonist or antagonist. But it's more likely to serve as a moment of possibility, a new threat that tells your reader, "These characters aren't as safe as they thought they were," paving a pathway for the next book in your series.

"We're Never Coming Back Here"

SCENARIO

Your protagonist and a group of loved ones have been trapped in a haunted house or castle for the weekend. Maybe they came here for a bachelorette party, or a fortieth birthday blowout, or a family reunion. Someone accidentally freed a demon trapped in an ancient relic, or they ignored the "Do Not Disturb" sign on the basement door and accidentally released a vampire who had been asleep for hundreds of years, or they've been fighting off alien critters. Whatever their antagonist was, they've vanquished it. Time to go home.

BRAINSTORM

Who survived the weekend? Who emerged as the leader/protector of the group? Who is the most broken? Think about where each of these characters began and how much they've changed in these few short days. This is not the type of experience you ever move on from. They will always think of their lives in two segments: before and after that fateful weekend.

WRITE

Write a scene where they finally escape, leaving this terrible place for good, but on their way out they realize someone's missing. One of your characters goes back to check on them, and *boom*. Whatever terror they faced inside takes one last victim.

OPTIONAL ELEMENTS TO INCLUDE

- Paramedics or other emergency services.
- A tearful call home.
- Another character goes to save the one who just died—and he dies too.

Callbacks

This scene might mirror the beginning of your novel, but these characters are shells of the people they were when they first arrived. You might echo some of the dialogue from the opening scenes, but now that the characters have lost so much their words take on new meaning.

“You Thought You Were Done with Me?”

SCENARIO

Your protagonist has been terrorized by a demonic, supernatural entity, but he finally killed the beast. Now he's driving home, exhausted but alive. That's what he keeps reminding himself: *I'm alive*. And there are so many people who aren't. Maybe that's what he's thinking about when he sees a kindly old man on the side of the road holding out his thumb. What could it hurt to give this guy a ride? Wouldn't it be nice to have a little company after losing so many friends?

BRAINSTORM

What are powers of the demon this protagonist has faced? Let's say it can take on a human form (or it can possess people, recklessly taking one body after another for a spin as it wreaks havoc on the world). What would give away the fact that this isn't a regular person? Is it a look in the demon's eyes? Can you hear it in its voice? How might your protagonist recognize it?

WRITE

Write a scene where your protagonist makes chitchat with a haunted hitchhiker who is secretly the demon in disguise. Build to a moment where your protagonist suddenly understands what's happening, then end the scene with a bang.

Remember: Your protagonist should see this coming, but he's let his guard down. He's too tired and relieved by what he thinks is his happy ending. You might want to let your readers see the demon first. Make them scream at the book in their hands, trying to warn your protagonist. But they're too late!

OPTIONAL ELEMENTS TO INCLUDE

- A portal to a hellish dimension.
- An explosion.
- Someone else is in the car with them.

Horror Twist

Instead of killing your protagonist, the demonic entity could take over his body. Your protagonist is the new vessel this demon will use as it sets out to cause more death and destruction. It's the worst fate your protagonist could ever imagine.

Callbacks

Make the most of the distinctive way this demonic entity speaks. At the beginning of the scene, you might have the hitchhiker sound human, but then let the demon's cadence slowly come out in a chilling reveal.

Look Behind You!

SCENARIO

A bogeyman has been stalking your characters. (Maybe it's similar to the Slender Man archetype: a faceless man with a hulking form who has a singular focus on his potential victims, cold-bloodedly stalking and killing them.) Your protagonist and one other surviving character have moved to a new city and taken on new identities. They're free.

BRAINSTORM

Think about how traumatic it would be to lose all your friends at the hands of a madman. How might these characters bogeyman-proof their home to ensure they never get terrorized again?

WRITE

Write a scene where these two characters finally let their guards down and enjoy themselves. Maybe they go to a carnival to play some games, or maybe they just have a quiet picnic in the park. Then one of them looks up and the monster's there. You don't even need to describe what happens next. Your readers will know.

OPTIONAL ELEMENTS TO INCLUDE

- They hear the bogeyman before they see him.
- A stranger gets in the bogeyman's way.
- Acceptance.

Horror Twist

This final scare should have the air of inevitability. These two characters might not even run. What's the point in running if you know the running won't ever stop?

Quick Writes

Set a timer for 15 minutes and do not stop writing until the timer goes off. Do not edit, cross out, or censor yourself. Write down every thought that comes to you.

1. After being terrorized by a ghost or evil entity, everyone believes your protagonist didn't make it. Write One Last Scare during their funeral when you reveal he isn't dead yet. He opens his eyes in the coffin. He's being buried alive . . .
2. Your protagonist and her friends managed to close a portal to hell. They saved the world. Write One Last Scare where an unknowing bystander accidentally reopens the portal. Maybe it's the end of the world after all.
3. Your protagonist uses a hatchet to destroy a demonic doll, shredding it to bits. Write One Last Scare where the demonic doll's spirit inhabits the hatchet. Chop, chop, chop!
4. After killing his Evil Twin, your protagonist reunites with an estranged partner. Their relationship was nearly ruined by the Evil Twin, but now they can have their happy ending. Write One Last Scare where you reveal that your protagonist isn't your protagonist at all—he's the Evil Twin in disguise.
5. Write One Last Scare where your protagonist and her friend finally flee a monster and make it to safety. As they embrace, the friend vanishes. Twist: She died earlier in the story, but your protagonist couldn't face that loss, so she's been imagining her friend until now.